Good Housekeeping

COMFORT
FOOD!

Barley Minestrone (recipe page 29)

Good Housekeeping

COMFORT FOOD!

SCRUMPTIOUS CLASSICS MADE EASY

HEARST BOOKS

New York

HEARST BOOKS
New York

An Imprint of Sterling Publishing
387 Park Avenue South
New York, NY 10016

GOOD HOUSEKEEPING

Rosemary Ellis
EDITOR IN CHIEF

Courtney Murphy
CREATIVE DIRECTOR

Susan Westmoreland
FOOD DIRECTOR

Samantha B. Cassetty, M.S., R.D.
NUTRITION DIRECTOR

Sharon Franke
FOOD APPLIANCES DIRECTOR

BOOK DESIGN by Memo Productions
PROJECT EDITOR Sarah Scheffel
Photography Credits on page 158

Library of Congress
Cataloging-in-Publication Data
Good Housekeeping comfort food! : scrumptious classics made easy.
    p. cm.
  ISBN 978-1-58816-884-9
1. Comfort food. 2. Cookbooks. I. Good House-keeping Institute (New York, N.Y.)
  TX714.G66135 2012
  641.3--dc22

                        2010054371

10 9 8 7 6 5 4 3 2 1

The Good Housekeeping Cookbook Seal guarantees that the recipes in this cookbook meet the strict standards of the Good Housekeeping Research Institute. The Institute has been a source of reliable information and a consumer advocate since 1900, and established its seal of approval in 1909. Every recipe has been triple-tested for ease, reliability, and great taste.

Published by Hearst Books
A division of Sterling Publishing Co., Inc.
387 Park Avenue South, New York, NY 10016

Good Housekeeping is a registered trademark of Hearst Communications, Inc.

www.goodhousekeeping.com

For information about custom editions, special sales, premium and corporate purchases, please contact Sterling Special Sales Department at 800-805-5489 or specialsales@sterlingpublishing.com.

Distributed in Canada by Sterling Publishing
c/o Canadian Manda Group, 165 Dufferin Street
Toronto, Ontario, Canada M6K 3H6

Distributed in Australia by Capricorn Link
(Australia) Pty. Ltd.
P.O. Box 704, Windsor, NSW 2756 Australia

Manufactured in China

Sterling ISBN 978-1-58816-884-9

CONTENTS

Lemon Ricotta Cheesecake (recipe page 146)

FOREWORD

Need a soothing dinner after a hard day at the office? Want a simple and hearty dish for a get-together with old friends? A bit of help to recreate a childhood favorite for your sister on her birthday? All of these occasions are perfect for warm-your-heart comfort food. For many of us, these favorites recall the dishes Mom (or maybe grandma) used to make—old-fashioned mac and cheese, succulent roast chicken, a side of mashed potatoes, or a slice of apple pie. One bite of these soothing classics and the world instantly feels like a kinder, cozier place.

At *Good Housekeeping* serving up family-pleasing comfort food has always been part of our mission. Here, we share our sure-to-satisfy picks, including Chicken Noodle Soup, Classic Beef Stew, and other warming soup-pot and slow-cooker dishes; piping-hot casseroles like Salsa Verde Enchiladas and Chili Pot Pie with Polenta Crust; plus Creamed Spinach, Potato Gratin with Gruyère, and other beloved sides perfect for holidays or everyday. If all this sounds waistline expanding, take heart: We've mixed in our healthy (and delicious!) makeovers of popular comfort food with fewer calories and less fat than the original versions. Enjoy a Curried Sweet Potato Shepherd's Pie made with heart-healthy ground turkey instead of beef, a Corn and Black Bean Tortilla Pie that melts reduced-fat cheese, and even a healthier French toast that swaps in low-fat milk and egg whites for some of the eggs so you can dig in without guilt!

And, of course, we haven't forgotten desserts: From our favorite oatmeal cookie (complete with chocolate *and* raisins) to Dark Chocolate–Walnut Caramel Pie to Vanilla Crème Brûlée, there's a treat to satisfy every craving.

SUSAN WESTMORELAND
Food Director, *Good Housekeeping*

INTRODUCTION

When the mood for comfort food strikes, you'll want to have basic ingredients and tools, and know how best to store extras—that is, if there are any leftovers! Here are good ideas to make sure you're ready.

Comfort food relies on a variety of perishable ingredients for its rich flavor: butter, milk, cream, eggs, cheeses—and don't forget the bacon! But stocking up on the following pantry ingredients will help ensure that you have what you need when it's time to cook.

STOCK YOUR PANTRY

• **Canned beans:** From kidney beans to cannellini, you'll want a selection on hand for soups, stews, and even brunch favorites like Huevos Rancheros (page 123).

• **Canned tomatoes, tomato paste:** A must for pasta dishes, including our crowd-pleasing Sausage and Pepper Baked Ziti (page 64).

• **Marinara sauce:** We provide an Easy Tomato Sauce recipe on page 52, but bottled marinara will come in handy again and again. If you want to make Hero Pizza (page 102) for movie night, you'll be ready.

• **Jarred salsa:** Beyond its obvious use as a dip for tortilla chips, we call for it in cozy dishes like Corn and Black Bean Tortilla Pie (page 98). Mild, medium, or hot—you decide.

- **Canned chicken and vegetable broth:** This is the basis for everything from soups and stews to slow-cooker dinners. We include recipes for homemade (pages 16 and 17), but it's smart to have canned on hand for ease.
- **Dried pasta:** Stock a range of shapes and sizes in your pantry, including some whole-wheat options. Those will come in handy for Penne Genovese with White Beans and Pesto (page 55), or any time you want to incorporate healthy whole grains in your comfort food.
- **Cornmeal:** If this isn't a staple in your pantry it should be. You'll need it for Chili Pot Pie with Polenta Crust (page 82) and other soul-satisfying dinners.
- **Chocolate chips, baking chocolate, cocoa powder:** Keep an arsenal of chocolate at the ready for all your baking needs. Cocoa Brownies with Mini Chocolate Chips (page 139) are best made with minis, though you could substitute standard ones in a pinch.
- **Ice cream, sorbet:** Keep vanilla on stand-by to pair with Easiest-Ever Apple Pie (page 144) and other favorite desserts.

TIME-SAVING APPLIANCES

This basic equipment will help you prepare piping hot entrées and delectable sweet treats with ease.

- Food processor with changeable cutting disks for chopping, slicing, and shredding.
- Immersion blender for pureeing soups and making gravies, dips, and sauces.
- Microwave oven for defrosting frozen meats, fish, and poultry; pre-cooking ingredients that take a long time to cook, such as potatoes and winter squash; reheating leftovers; steaming vegetables; melting butter and cheese.
- Ridged grill pan to make it easy to grill indoors in your kitchen. It uses very little oil, preheats fast, and leaves the familiar grill marks on the food.
- Slow cooker for soups, stews, poultry and meat casseroles, and even lasagna! It allows you to prep, set, and forget—then enjoy a hot homemade dinner at the end of a long day. For tips, see Slow-Cooker Success (page 35).

SAFE NONSTICK COOKING

Easy to clean and very popular, nonstick skillets are the go-to pan for many comfort foods. Just follow these cooking guidelines to keep your pans safe and in good shape.

1 Never preheat an empty nonstick pan, even one with oil in it.

2 Don't cook over high heat. Most nonstick manufacturers now advise consumers not to go above medium. (The coating may begin to break down at temperatures over 500°F.)

3 Ventilate your kitchen. When cooking, turn on the exhaust fan to help clear away any fumes.

4 Don't broil or sear meats in a nonstick pan. Those techniques require temperatures above what nonstick can usually handle.

5 Choose a heavier nonstick pan. Lightweight pans generally heat up fastest; heavier cookware is worth the extra money.

6 Avoid scratching or chipping the pan. Use wooden spoons for stirring, don't use steel wool for cleaning, and don't stack the pans when you store them. (If you do, place a paper towel between them.)

IS IT DONE YET?

Our recipes provide cooking times and visual cues, but here are some general tips on how to know when a dish is done.

• **Stews and pot roasts:** Beef, pork, lamb, and other meats in braised dishes need to cook longer to break down the connective tissue, whether you're using the oven or a slow cooker. To test: Insert a fork into the meat. If it's tender throughout, and pulls apart with no resistance, it's done.

• **Pasta:** Forget about throwing spaghetti against the wall; if it sticks, it's overcooked. To test: Do as the Italians do and take a taste. Start taste-testing early, two-thirds of the way through the cooking time. The pasta should be *al dente*—tender but still firm and chewy.

• **Chicken breasts:** Boneless chicken breasts are a great lean choice, but are easy to overcook. They should end up moist and juicy, not dried out. To test: Insert an instant-read thermometer horizontally at the thicker end of the breast, and stop cooking when it reads 165°F. Or pierce the breast with the tip of a sharp knife; if the juices run clear, it's done.

• **Green vegetables:** There's a fine line between undercooking and overcooking green veggies, especially if you're steaming or boiling. Check them first after they've cooked 3 to 4 minutes to see if they're getting close. Broccoli, green beans, snow peas, asparagus, and the like, should be tender but still have a bit of crispness. To test: Pierce one piece with the tip of a sharp knife, or take a small bite—it should resist just slightly. (To stop cooking and maintain color, rinse with cold water immediately after draining.)

- **Sweet and savory pies:** A beautifully browned crust isn't always the best indicator of doneness. To test: Check the filling. Fruit pies and pot pies are ready to come out of the oven when the filling bubbles through the openings or slits in the crust. For custard pies, like pumpkin, insert a knife 2 inches from the crust's edge—if it comes out clean, the pie is ready.

FREEZE WITH EASE

Many of the stews, casseroles, and pies in this book are perfect candidates for freezing. Make two and freeze one for double-duty dinners you can enjoy on a busy weeknight.

TO FREEZE

Before freezing, refrigerate soups or stews for 30 minutes. Casseroles need 30 minutes at room temperature plus 30 minutes in the fridge before they can be transferred to the freezer. Wrap casseroles tightly in foil or plastic wrap. Seal soups and stews in zip-tight plastic bags or freezer containers, which are usually made from thicker plastic. To maximize space, stack bags horizontally until frozen, then store upright. Or line your baking dish with heavy-duty greased foil before making the casserole; once the meal is frozen solid, remove the frozen food and transfer it to a large zip-tight plastic bag.

TO THAW

STEWS, SOUPS, AND CHILIS

Place frozen food, still sealed in a plastic bag, in a bowl or sink of hot water for 5 to 10 minutes or until it can be broken into pieces. If the food is in a sealed freezer-weight container, leave it in hot water until the food separates from its sides. Open the bag or container; invert contents into a saucepan (for stovetop heating) or into a microwave-safe bowl.

CASSEROLES AND PIES

At least 24 hours but no more than 2 days before reheating, refrigerate the frozen casserole to thaw slightly. If the casserole was frozen in a foil-lined baking dish and then removed from the dish for storage, unwrap it and slip it back into the baking dish to thaw.

TO REHEAT

STEWS, SOUPS, AND CHILIS ON A STOVETOP

Add ¼ to ½ cup water to the saucepan to prevent scorching. Cover and heat to boiling over medium heat, then boil 1 minute to be sure it's fully heated; stir frequently throughout the process.

CASSEROLES IN A CONVENTIONAL OVEN

Unwrap the frozen casserole; loosely cover it with foil, and bake about 1 hour, then uncover and bake 20 to 30 minutes longer or until the center of the casserole reaches 160°F on an instant-read thermometer.

CASSEROLES, SOUPS, STEWS, AND CHILIS IN A MICROWAVE

Don't remove the carousel in your microwave to accommodate large casseroles—a microwave that rotates food won't do its job without turning. Unwrap the casserole; cover the top of the microwave-safe dish with waxed paper or plastic wrap and turn back a corner to vent. Put soups, stews, and chilis in a microwave-safe bowl and cover with waxed paper or vented plastic wrap. Note: Do not allow plastic wrap to touch food during microwaving because it may melt.

Heat casseroles about 30 minutes in microwave; heat soups, stews, and chilis about 10 minutes, first on Low (30%) until ice crystals are gone and you can easily insert a knife into center of casserole, or can stir soup, stew, or chili. Then heat on High 5 to 15 minutes longer, until food is heated through, and the internal temperature of your casserole is 160°F.

COZY SOUPS & STEWS

Here's TLC by the spoonful: Enjoy a steaming bowl as a starter, or add some bread for an easy supper. Choose from comforting favorites like chicken noodle, clam chowder, and beef stew, or try our twists on classics including a minestrone made with barley and a borscht of grated beets and cabbage in a light broth. An added bonus for the cook: Soups often taste even better the next day, which means leftovers are sure to be satisfying.

Canned broth is a great timesaver, but our recipes for veggie and chicken stock make homemade soups extra flavorful. Consider preparing a batch of broth ahead of time and freezing it so you always have it on hand.

Not Your Grandmother's Borscht (recipe page 28)

HOMEMADE VEGETABLE BROTH

This broth is delicious and nutritious. The optional fennel and parsnip lend a natural sweetness and an additional depth of flavor.

ACTIVE TIME: 25 MINUTES · TOTAL TIME: 2 HOURS 25 MINUTES
MAKES: ABOUT 6 CUPS

4   LARGE LEEKS

2 TO 4 GARLIC CLOVES, NOT PEELED

13 CUPS WATER

SALT

1   LARGE ALL-PURPOSE POTATO, PEELED, CUT LENGTHWISE IN HALF, AND THINLY SLICED

1   SMALL FENNEL BULB, TRIMMED AND CHOPPED (OPTIONAL)

3   PARSNIPS, PEELED AND THINLY SLICED (OPTIONAL)

2   LARGE CARROTS, PEELED AND THINLY SLICED

3   STALKS CELERY WITH LEAVES, THINLY SLICED

4   OUNCES MUSHROOMS, TRIMMED AND THINLY SLICED

10 PARSLEY SPRIGS

4   THYME SPRIGS

2   BAY LEAVES

1   TEASPOON WHOLE BLACK PEPPERCORNS

GROUND BLACK PEPPER

1   Cut off roots and trim dark green tops from leeks; thinly slice leeks. Rinse leeks in large bowl of cold water, swishing to remove sand. Transfer to colander to drain, leaving sand in bottom of bowl.

2   In 6-quart saucepot, combine leeks, garlic, 1 cup water, and pinch salt; heat to boiling. Reduce heat to medium; cover and cook until leeks are tender, about 15 minutes.

3   Add potato, fennel if using, parsnips if using, carrots, celery, mushrooms, parsley and thyme sprigs, bay leaves, peppercorns, and remaining 12 cups water. Heat to boiling; reduce heat and simmer, uncovered, at least 1 hour 30 minutes.

4   Taste and continue cooking if flavor is not concentrated enough. Season with salt and pepper to taste. Strain broth through fine-mesh sieve into containers, pressing on solids with back of wooden spoon to extract liquid; cool. Cover and refrigerate to use within 3 days, or freeze up to 4 months.

EACH CUP: ABOUT 20 CALORIES | 1G PROTEIN | 4G CARBOHYDRATE | 0G TOTAL FAT (0G SATURATED) | 0MG CHOLESTEROL | 9MG SODIUM

HOMEMADE CHICKEN BROTH

Nothing beats the rich flavor of homemade chicken broth. Our recipe has an added bonus: The cooked chicken can be used in casseroles and salads. Make it or the veggie broth, opposite, in large batches and freeze in sturdy containers for up to four months. If you're in a hurry and want to use canned broth, one 14-ounce can equals 1¾ cups broth.

ACTIVE TIME: 30 MINUTES · TOTAL TIME: 4 HOURS 40 MINUTES PLUS COOLING
MAKES: ABOUT 5½ CUPS

1 CHICKEN (3 TO 3½ POUNDS), INCLUDING NECK (RESERVE GIBLETS FOR ANOTHER USE)

2 CARROTS, PEELED AND CUT INTO 2-INCH PIECES

1 STALK CELERY, CUT INTO 2-INCH PIECES

1 MEDIUM ONION, UNPEELED, CUT INTO QUARTERS

5 PARSLEY SPRIGS

1 GARLIC CLOVE, UNPEELED

½ TEASPOON DRIED THYME

½ BAY LEAF

3 QUARTS WATER PLUS MORE IF NEEDED

1 In 6-quart saucepot, combine chicken, chicken neck, carrots, celery, onion, parsley, garlic, thyme, bay leaf, and water. If necessary, add more water to cover broth ingredients; heat to boiling over high heat. With slotted spoon, skim foam from surface. Reduce heat to low; cover and simmer, turning chicken once and skimming foam occasionally, 1 hour.

2 Remove from heat; transfer chicken to large bowl. When chicken is cool enough to handle, remove skin and bones and reserve meat for another use. Return skin and bones to pot and heat to boiling over high heat. Skim foam; reduce heat to low and simmer, uncovered, 3 hours.

3 Strain broth through colander into large bowl; discard solids. Strain again through fine-mesh sieve into containers; cool. Cover and refrigerate to use within 3 days, or freeze up to 4 months.

4 Skim and discard fat from surface of broth before use.

EACH CUP: ABOUT 35 CALORIES | 3G PROTEIN | 4G CARBOHYDRATE | 1G TOTAL FAT (1G SATURATED) | 3MG CHOLESTEROL | 91MG SODIUM

CHICKEN NOODLE SOUP

For old-fashioned flavor with a minimum of fuss, try this hearty version of the cozy classic. Although it's not traditional, a squeeze of fresh lemon will brighten the flavors.

ACTIVE TIME: 10 MINUTES · TOTAL TIME: 25 MINUTES
MAKES: 5 MAIN-DISH SERVINGS

4 CUPS CHICKEN BROTH (TO MAKE HOMEMADE, SEE PAGE 17)

4 CUPS WATER

1 TABLESPOON OLIVE OIL

1 SMALL ONION, CHOPPED

2 STALKS CELERY, THINLY SLICED

2 MEDIUM CARROTS, PEELED AND THINLY SLICED

¼ TEASPOON GROUND BLACK PEPPER

1 POUND SKINLESS, BONELESS CHICKEN-BREAST HALVES

3 CUPS MEDIUM EGG NOODLES, UNCOOKED (6 OUNCES)

1 CUP FROZEN PEAS, THAWED

1   In covered 3-quart saucepan, heat broth and water over high heat.

2   Meanwhile, in 5- to 6-quart saucepot, heat oil over medium heat. Add onion and cook, stirring occasionally, until onion is lightly browned, about 5 minutes. Add celery, carrots, hot broth mixture, and pepper; cover saucepot and heat to boiling over high heat.

3   While vegetables are cooking, cut chicken into ¾-inch pieces.

4   Uncover saucepot and stir in egg noodles; cover and cook 3 minutes. Stir in peas and chicken; cover and heat to boiling, 3 to 4 minutes.

EACH SERVING: ABOUT 305 CALORIES | 30G PROTEIN | 33G CARBOHYDRATE | 6G TOTAL FAT (1G SATURATED) | 3G FIBER | 85MG CHOLESTEROL | 615MG SODIUM

BLACK BEAN AND CHICKEN TORTILLA SOUP

This satisfying chicken soup has three major players: black beans, golden browned chicken thighs, and spicy Mexican-style seasonings.

ACTIVE TIME: 30 MINUTES · TOTAL TIME: 1 HOUR 5 MINUTES
MAKES: 8 MAIN-DISH SERVINGS

1   TABLESPOON VEGETABLE OIL

1½ POUNDS BONELESS, SKINLESS CHICKEN THIGHS, CUT INTO ½-INCH-WIDE STRIPS

½   TEASPOON SALT

1   LARGE ONION (12 OUNCES), CHOPPED

2   MEDIUM POBLANO CHILES (3 OUNCES EACH), SEEDED AND CHOPPED

2   GARLIC CLOVES, CRUSHED WITH GARLIC PRESS

1½ TEASPOONS GROUND CUMIN

1   TEASPOON GROUND CORIANDER

4   CUPS REDUCED-SODIUM CHICKEN BROTH (TO MAKE HOMEMADE, WHICH IS NATURALLY LOW IN SODIUM, SEE PAGE 17)

2   CUPS WATER

1   CUP FROZEN CORN KERNELS

32 OUNCES BLACK BEANS, RINSED AND DRAINED (ABOUT 2 CANS)

¼   CUP FRESH LIME JUICE

¼   CUP LOOSELY PACKED FRESH CILANTRO LEAVES, CHOPPED

2   CUPS COARSELY BROKEN TORTILLA CHIPS

1   In 6-quart saucepot, heat oil over medium-high heat until hot.

2   Sprinkle chicken with salt. Add chicken to saucepot in 2 batches and cook, stirring occasionally, until lightly browned, about 5 minutes per batch. With slotted spoon, transfer chicken to medium bowl.

3   After all chicken is browned, add onion, poblanos, and garlic to saucepot; cook over medium heat, stirring occasionally, until vegetables are lightly browned and tender, about 10 minutes. Stir in cumin and coriander; cook 1 minute. Add broth and water; cover and heat to boiling.

4   Return chicken, and any juices in bowl, to pot; stir in corn and beans. Heat to boiling over medium-high heat; reduce heat to medium-low and simmer, uncovered, 10 minutes to blend flavors. Stir in lime juice and cilantro.

5   Ladle soup into bowls. Serve with tortilla chips to sprinkle on top of soup.

EACH SERVING: ABOUT 240 CALORIES | 22G PROTEIN | 25G CARBOHYDRATE | 7G TOTAL FAT (1G SATURATED) | 5G FIBER | 71MG CHOLESTEROL | 625MG SODIUM

CLASSIC BEEF STEW

Meat and potatoes reach their full potential in this hearty stew.

ACTIVE TIME: 45 MINUTES · TOTAL TIME: 2 HOURS 45 MINUTES
MAKES: 8 MAIN-DISH SERVINGS

- 2   POUNDS BONELESS BEEF CHUCK, TRIMMED OF FAT AND CUT INTO 1½-INCH PIECES
- 4   TEASPOONS OLIVE OIL
- 1   LARGE ONION (12 OUNCES), CHOPPED
- 2   GARLIC CLOVES, FINELY CHOPPED
- 1   CAN (14 OUNCES) DICED TOMATOES
- 2   CUPS DRY RED WINE
- 1   BAY LEAF
- 1   TEASPOON SALT
- ¼   TEASPOON GROUND BLACK PEPPER
- ¼   TEASPOON DRIED THYME
- 1½ POUNDS POTATOES, PEELED AND CUT INTO 1½-INCH PIECES
- 6   CARROTS, PEELED AND CUT INTO 1-INCH PIECES
- 1   CUP FROZEN PEAS
- 2   TABLESPOONS CHOPPED FRESH PARSLEY LEAVES

1   Preheat oven to 325°F. Pat beef dry with paper towels. In 6-quart Dutch oven, heat 2 teaspoons oil over medium-high heat until very hot. Add half of beef and cook 5 minutes or until well browned on all sides. Transfer beef to large bowl. Add remaining 2 teaspoons oil to Dutch oven and repeat with remaining beef.

2   Reduce heat to medium. Add onion to Dutch oven and cook, stirring occasionally, until tender, about 5 minutes. Add garlic and cook 30 seconds or until very fragrant. Stir in tomatoes with their juices. Add wine, bay leaf, salt, pepper, thyme, and beef with its accumulated juices. Heat to boiling over high heat.

3   Cover and transfer to oven. Cook 1 hour. Add potatoes and carrots; cook 1 hour longer or until vegetables are fork-tender. Discard bay leaf.

4   With a slotted spoon, transfer vegetables and beef to bowl and cover with foil to keep warm. Skim and discard fat from cooking liquid.

5   Raise heat to medium-high and cook liquid until slightly reduced, 5 to 7 minutes. Stir in frozen peas and cook 1 to 2 minutes longer or until heated through. Spoon liquid and peas over meat mixture. Sprinkle with parsley.

EACH SERVING: ABOUT 290 CALORIES | 27G PROTEIN | 28G CARBOHYDRATE | 7G TOTAL FAT (2G SATURATED) | 5G FIBER | 48MG CHOLESTEROL | 450MG SODIUM

NEW ENGLAND CLAM CHOWDER

Clam chowder, New England's signature seafood dish, is always satisfying. To slim this dish without sacrificing flavor, we trimmed the bacon, swapped reduced-fat milk for cream, and stirred in flour to give it body.

ACTIVE TIME: 20 MINUTES · TOTAL TIME: 1 HOUR
MAKES: 6 FIRST-COURSE SERVINGS

1½ CUPS WATER

12 LARGE CHERRYSTONE OR CHOWDER CLAMS, SCRUBBED

2 SLICES BACON, CHOPPED

1 MEDIUM ONION, CHOPPED

1 MEDIUM CARROT, PEELED AND CHOPPED

1 STALK CELERY, CHOPPED

2 TABLESPOONS ALL-PURPOSE FLOUR

1 LARGE POTATO (12 OUNCES), PEELED AND CUT INTO ½-INCH PIECES

2 CUPS REDUCED-FAT MILK (2%)

⅛ TEASPOON GROUND BLACK PEPPER

1 TABLESPOON FINELY CHOPPED FRESH CHIVES

1 In 4-quart saucepan, heat water to boiling over high heat. Add clams; heat to boiling. Reduce heat to medium-low; cover and simmer 10 minutes or until clams open, transferring clams to bowl as they open. Discard any unopened clams.

2 Into 4-cup liquid measuring cup, strain clam broth through sieve lined with paper towel. Add *water* to broth to equal 2½ cups total.

3 Rinse saucepan to remove any grit. In same saucepan, cook bacon over medium heat until browned. With slotted spoon, transfer bacon to paper towels to drain. To bacon fat in pan, add onion, carrot, and celery; cook, stirring occasionally, until tender, 9 to 10 minutes.

4 Meanwhile, remove clams from shells and coarsely chop.

5 Stir flour into vegetable mixture; cook 1 minute, stirring. Gradually stir in clam broth. Add potato and heat to boiling. Cover; simmer over low heat, stirring occasionally, until potato is tender, about 12 minutes. Stir in milk, clams, pepper, and bacon; heat through (do not boil). Sprinkle chowder with chives to serve.

EACH SERVING: ABOUT 180 CALORIES | 8G PROTEIN | 20G CARBOHYDRATE | 9G TOTAL FAT (4G SATURATED) | 2G FIBER | 21MG CHOLESTEROL | 155MG SODIUM

FRENCH ONION SOUP

Onions, slowly cooked until caramelized, give this classic its distinctive flavor. Gruyère melted on top of toasted bread provides the rich finish.

ACTIVE TIME: 10 MINUTES · TOTAL TIME: 2 HOURS
MAKES: 4 FIRST-COURSE SERVINGS

4 TABLESPOONS BUTTER OR MARGARINE	¼ TEASPOON DRIED THYME
6 MEDIUM ONIONS, THINLY SLICED	4 DIAGONAL SLICES (½-INCH THICK) FRENCH BREAD
¼ TEASPOON SALT	4 OUNCES GRUYÈRE OR SWISS CHEESE, SHREDDED (1 CUP)
4 CUPS WATER	
1 CAN (14 TO 14½ OUNCES) BEEF BROTH	

1   In nonstick 12-inch skillet, melt butter over medium-low heat. Add onions and salt and cook, stirring occasionally, until onions are very tender and begin to caramelize, about 45 minutes. Reduce heat to low and cook, stirring frequently, until onions are deep golden brown, about 15 minutes longer.

2   Transfer onions to 5-quart Dutch oven. Add ½ cup water to same skillet and heat to boiling, stirring until browned bits are loosened from bottom of skillet. Add to onions in Dutch oven. Add remaining 3½ cups water, broth, and thyme to onions and heat to boiling over high heat. Reduce heat and simmer 30 minutes.

3   Preheat oven to 450°F. Arrange bread slices on cookie sheet and bake until lightly toasted, about 5 minutes. Place four ovenproof bowls in jelly-roll pan for easier handling. Spoon soup evenly into bowls and top with toasted bread, slightly pressing bread into soup. Sprinkle Gruyère evenly on top. Bake until cheese has melted and begins to brown, 12 to 15 minutes.

EACH SERVING: ABOUT 400 CALORIES | 15G PROTEIN | 37G CARBOHYDRATE | 22G TOTAL FAT (13G SATURATED FAT) | 64MG CHOLESTEROL | 887MG SODIUM

WINTER VEGETABLE CHOWDER

This thyme-scented vegetable chowder boasts a creamy finish thanks to a dose of half-and-half.

ACTIVE TIME: 15 MINUTES · TOTAL TIME: 50 MINUTES
MAKES: 8 MAIN-DISH SERVINGS

6 MEDIUM LEEKS (3 POUNDS)	3½ CUPS VEGETABLE BROTH (TO MAKE HOMEMADE, SEE PAGE 16)
2 TABLESPOONS OLIVE OIL	
4 MEDIUM STALKS CELERY, CUT INTO ½-INCH SLICES	4 CUPS WATER
	½ TEASPOON CHOPPED FRESH THYME LEAVES PLUS THYME SPRIG FOR GARNISH
3 MEDIUM PARSNIPS, PEELED AND CHOPPED	
2 MEDIUM RED POTATOES (1 POUND), CUT INTO ½-INCH PIECES	1 TEASPOON SALT
	¾ TEASPOON GROUND BLACK PEPPER
2 CUPS (½-INCH PIECES) BUTTERNUT SQUASH (FROM 2 POUNDS SQUASH)	1 CUP HALF-AND-HALF OR LIGHT CREAM

1 Cut off roots and trim dark-green tops from leeks. Discard any tough outer leaves. Cut each leek lengthwise in half, then crosswise into ½-inch slices. Rinse in large bowl of cold water; swish to remove sand. With hands, transfer rinsed leeks to colander, leaving sand in bottom of bowl. Repeat rinsing and draining several times, until all sand is removed. Drain well.

2 In 6-quart saucepot, heat oil over medium-high heat until hot. Add leeks, celery, and parsnips and cook, stirring occasionally, until all vegetables are tender, 10 to 12 minutes.

3 Add potatoes, squash, broth, water, chopped thyme, salt, and pepper; heat to boiling over medium-high heat. Cover, then reduce heat to medium-low and simmer about 10 minutes or until vegetables are tender. Stir in half-and-half and heat through, about 3 minutes.

4 Spoon into tureen and garnish with thyme sprig.

TIP This chowder freezes especially well—enjoy one meal, then stash the leftovers for another day.

EACH SERVING: ABOUT 215 CALORIES | 5G PROTEIN | 35G CARBOHYDRATE | 8G TOTAL FAT (3G SATURATED) | 5G FIBER | 11MG CHOLESTEROL | 560MG SODIUM

NOT YOUR GRAND-MOTHER'S BORSCHT

Traditionally, borscht is a hearty peasant-style stew with chunks of beets, cabbage, and possibly some meat. Here we offer a more refined but equally comforting take on this Russian classic. Colorful grated beets and cabbage in a light vegetable broth are topped with a dollop of sour cream, if you like. For photo, see page 14.

ACTIVE TIME: 15 MINUTES · TOTAL TIME: 1 HOUR
MAKES: 5 MAIN-DISH SERVINGS

1 TABLESPOON OLIVE OIL	4 CUPS WATER
1 MEDIUM ONION, CHOPPED	2 CUPS VEGETABLE BROTH (TO MAKE HOMEMADE, SEE PAGE 16)
1 GARLIC CLOVE, CRUSHED WITH GARLIC PRESS	1 BAY LEAF
½ TEASPOON GROUND ALLSPICE	¾ TEASPOON SALT
1 CAN (14½ OUNCES) DICED TOMATOES	2 TABLESPOONS RED WINE VINEGAR
1 POUND BEETS	¼ CUP LOOSELY PACKED FRESH DILL OR PARSLEY, CHOPPED
6 CUPS SLICED GREEN CABBAGE (1 POUND)	REDUCED-FAT SOUR CREAM (OPTIONAL)
3 LARGE CARROTS, PEELED AND CUT INTO ½-INCH PIECES	

1 In 5- to 6-quart saucepot, heat oil over medium heat until hot. Add onion and cook 8 minutes or until tender. Stir in garlic and allspice; cook 30 seconds. Add tomatoes and cook 5 minutes.

2 Meanwhile, cut off the tops then peel beets (see Tip) and shred them in food processor (or on the coarse side of box grater).

3 Into saucepot with onion mixture, stir shredded beets, cabbage, carrots, water, broth, bay leaf, and salt; heat to boiling over high heat.

4 Reduce heat to medium-low; cover and simmer about 30 minutes or until all vegetables are tender. Remove bay leaf. Stir in vinegar and dill. Serve with sour cream, if desired.

TIP Wear rubber gloves while peeling beets for easier cleanup.

EACH SERVING: ABOUT 160 CALORIES | 5G PROTEIN | 27G CARBOHYDRATE | 5G TOTAL FAT (1G SATURATED) | 6G FIBER | 5MG CHOLESTEROL | 920MG SODIUM

BARLEY MINESTRONE

This minestrone is bursting with grains and veggies. A dollop of pesto and sprinkling of Pecorino makes it irresistible. For photo, see page 2.

ACTIVE TIME: 25 MINUTES · **TOTAL TIME:** 1 HOUR 15 MINUTES
MAKES: 6 MAIN-DISH SERVINGS

1 CUP PEARL BARLEY

3 TABLESPOONS OLIVE OIL

2 CUPS THINLY SLICED GREEN CABBAGE (ABOUT ½ SMALL HEAD)

2 LARGE CARROTS, PEELED, EACH CUT LENGTHWISE IN HALF, THEN CROSSWISE INTO ½-INCH-THICK SLICES

2 LARGE STALKS CELERY, CUT INTO ½-INCH SLICES

1 MEDIUM ONION, CUT INTO ½-INCH CUBES

1 GARLIC CLOVE, FINELY CHOPPED

3 CUPS WATER

3½ CUPS VEGETABLE BROTH (TO MAKE HOMEMADE, SEE PAGE 16)

1 CAN (14½ OUNCES) DICED TOMATOES

¼ TEASPOON SALT

1 MEDIUM ZUCCHINI, CUT INTO ½-INCH CUBES

1 CUP GREEN BEANS, CUT INTO ½-INCH PIECES (ABOUT ¼ POUND)

FRESHLY GRATED PECORINO-ROMANO CHEESE OR STORE-BOUGHT PESTO (OPTIONAL)

1 Heat 6-quart Dutch oven over medium-high heat until hot. Add barley. Cook, stirring constantly, until toasted and fragrant, 3 to 4 minutes. Transfer barley to small bowl; set aside.

2 In same Dutch oven, heat 1 tablespoon oil over medium-high heat until hot. Add cabbage, carrots, celery, and onion; cook, stirring occasionally, until vegetables are tender and lightly browned, 8 to 10 minutes. Add garlic and cook 30 seconds longer, or until fragrant. Stir in toasted barley, water, broth, tomatoes, and salt. Cover Dutch oven and heat to boiling over high heat. Reduce heat to low and simmer, covered, for 25 minutes.

3 Stir zucchini and beans into vegetable-barley mixture; increase heat to medium and cook, covered, 10 to 15 minutes or until all vegetables and barley are tender.

4 Ladle minestrone into 6 large soup bowls (see Tip). Top with Pecorino or pesto, if desired.

TIP If you like, warm bowls in a 200°F oven before you ladle in the soup.

EACH SERVING: ABOUT 215 CALORIES | 7G PROTEIN | 42G CARBOHYDRATE | 4G TOTAL FAT (0G SATURATED) | 9G FIBER | 0MG CHOLESTEROL | 690MG SODIUM

ZUCCHINI AND PEPPER CIAMBOTTA

This main-dish vegetable stew also makes a delicious accompaniment to roasted chicken, fish, or meat.

ACTIVE TIME: 15 MINUTES · TOTAL TIME: 1 HOUR
MAKES: 6 MAIN-DISH SERVINGS

2   TABLESPOONS EXTRA-VIRGIN OLIVE OIL

1   LARGE ONION (12 OUNCES), CHOPPED

2   SMALL BULBS FENNEL (ABOUT 1 POUND EACH), TRIMMED OF STEMS AND TOUGH OUTER LAYERS, THINLY SLICED

1   LARGE RED PEPPER, CUT INTO 1-INCH PIECES

3   GARLIC CLOVES, FINELY CHOPPED

1   CAN (28 OUNCES) WHOLE TOMATOES IN JUICE

4   MEDIUM ZUCCHINI, CUT INTO ½-INCH PIECES

1   POUND GREEN BEANS, TRIMMED AND CUT INTO 1-INCH PIECES

½   TEASPOON SALT

⅔   CUP LOOSELY PACKED FRESH BASIL LEAVES, THINLY SLICED

1   In 5- to 6-quart Dutch oven, heat oil over medium heat until hot. Add onion and fennel; cook 15 minutes or until vegetables are lightly browned and tender, stirring occasionally. Add red pepper and garlic and cook 5 minutes or until pepper is tender-crisp.

2   Add tomatoes with juice, zucchini, green beans, and salt; heat to boiling over medium-high heat, stirring and breaking up tomatoes with side of spoon. Reduce heat to medium-low; cover and simmer 30 minutes or until vegetables are very tender. Stir in all but 2 tablespoons basil; top with remaining basil to serve.

EACH SERVING: ABOUT 160 CALORIES | 6G PROTEIN | 28G CARBOHYDRATE | 6G TOTAL FAT (1G SATURATED) | 10G FIBER | 0MG CHOLESTEROL | 430MG SODIUM

SLOW-COOKER DINNERS

The slow cooker is a natural choice for comfort food. Its low and slow method encourages meats to become meltingly tender, vegetables to fully absorb stocks and spices, and flavors to develop to their fullest.

Here we offer a sampling of one-pot perfection: a lazy coq au vin and Latin-style chicken with black beans and sweet potatoes, a luscious lamb tagine and a simple lentil and squash stew. There's even a recipe for lasagna you can make—from start to finish—in your slow cooker. For optimum results, see Slow-Cooker Success, page 35.

Lamb and Root Vegetable Tagine (recipe page 43)

CHICKEN WITH BEANS AND SWEET POTATOES

This spicy, smoky Latin chicken dish requires just 15 minutes of prep time, so it's easy to throw together in the morning.

ACTIVE TIME: 15 MINUTES · **SLOW-COOK TIME:** 8 HOURS ON LOW OR 4 HOURS ON HIGH
MAKES: 6 MAIN-DISH SERVINGS

3   POUNDS BONE-IN SKINLESS CHICKEN THIGHS

2   TEASPOONS GROUND CUMIN

¼   TEASPOON SALT

¼   TEASPOON GROUND BLACK PEPPER

1   TEASPOON SMOKED PAPRIKA

½   TEASPOON GROUND ALLSPICE

1   CUP CHICKEN BROTH (TO MAKE HOMEMADE, SEE PAGE 17)

½   CUP SALSA

3   LARGE GARLIC CLOVES, CRUSHED WITH GARLIC PRESS

2   CANS (16 OUNCES EACH) BLACK BEANS, RINSED AND DRAINED

2   POUNDS SWEET POTATOES, PEELED AND CUT INTO 2-INCH PIECES

1   JARRED ROASTED RED PEPPER, CUT INTO STRIPS (1 CUP)

⅓   CUP LOOSELY PACKED FRESH CILANTRO LEAVES, CHOPPED

LIME WEDGES

1 Sprinkle chicken thighs with ½ teaspoon cumin, salt, and pepper. Heat nonstick 12-inch skillet over medium heat until hot; add chicken and cook until well browned on all sides, 10 to 12 minutes. Transfer chicken to plate. Remove skillet from heat.

2 In the same skillet, combine smoked paprika, allspice, broth, salsa, garlic, and remaining 1½ teaspoons cumin.

3 In 6- to 6½ quart slow-cooker bowl, combine beans and sweet potatoes. Place chicken on top of sweet-potato mixture in slow cooker; pour broth mixture over chicken. Cover slow cooker and cook on Low 8 hours or on High 4 hours.

4 With tongs or slotted spoon, remove chicken pieces to large platter. Gently stir red pepper strips into sweet-potato mixture, then spoon mixture over chicken. Sprinkle with cilantro and serve with lime wedges.

EACH SERVING: ABOUT 415 CALORIES | 36G PROTEIN | 61G CARBOHYDRATE | 6G TOTAL FAT (1G SATURATED) | 12G FIBER | 107MG CHOLESTEROL | 875MG SODIUM

SLOW-COOKER SUCCESS

Here are tips to ensure you get the most out of your slow cooker.

1 Prep the night before, and all you'll need to do in the morning is toss your ingredients into the slow-cooker bowl and flip the switch. (Measure ingredients, cut veggies, and trim fat from meats, then refrigerate components separately in bowls or storage bags so, for instance, the acid in wine doesn't change the texture of the meat.)

2 Less tender cuts of meat and poultry—such as pork and lamb shoulder, chuck roast, beef brisket, and poultry legs—are best suited for slow cooking. Skim fat from cooking liquid when done. (Fish and other seafood aren't a good option for the slow cooker unless added in the last hour of cooking.)

3 Slow cooking tends to intensify flavorful spices and seasonings such as chili powder and garlic, so use them conservatively.

4 Dried herbs may lessen in flavor, so adjust seasonings by stirring a little more in at the end of cooking. When using fresh herbs, save some to toss in at the last minute for fresh flavor and color.

5 For richer flavor in stews, sprinkle meat and poultry with flour and brown in skillet before slow cooking. (Scrape up browned bits in skillet and add to the pot to help thicken sauce and enhance flavor even more.)

6 Don't take the lid off the cooker to stir ingredients, especially in the early stages of warming—the pot will lose valuable heat.

EIGHT-HOUR COQ AU VIN

If you're an early riser with extra a.m. time, try this easy, make-ahead Coq au Vin. You can even cook extra bacon to munch on for breakfast.

ACTIVE TIME: 20 MINUTES · **SLOW-COOK TIME:** 8 HOURS ON LOW OR 4 HOURS ON HIGH
MAKES: 4 MAIN-DISH SERVINGS

---

3   SLICES BACON, CUT CROSSWISE INTO ¾-INCH PIECES

10 OUNCES MUSHROOMS, EACH CUT IN HALF

2   CUPS FROZEN PEARL ONIONS

1   CUT-UP CHICKEN (3½ TO 4 POUNDS), SKIN REMOVED FROM ALL PIECES EXCEPT WINGS

½   TEASPOON SALT

¼   TEASPOON GROUND BLACK PEPPER

1   MEDIUM ONION, CHOPPED

1   LARGE CARROT, PEELED AND CHOPPED

4   GARLIC CLOVES, CHOPPED

1   CUP DRY RED WINE

2   TABLESPOONS TOMATO PASTE

1   BAY LEAF

¾   CUP CHICKEN BROTH (TO MAKE HOMEMADE, SEE PAGE 17)

---

1 In nonstick 12-inch skillet, cook bacon over medium heat until browned. With slotted spoon, transfer bacon to paper towels to drain; set aside and refrigerate.

2 Meanwhile, in 5- to 6-quart slow-cooker bowl, combine mushrooms and pearl onions.

3 Sprinkle chicken pieces with salt and pepper. In skillet with bacon fat, cook chicken (in 2 batches, if necessary) over medium-high heat until browned, about 10 minutes. Place chicken over mushrooms and onions in slow cooker.

4 Discard drippings from skillet. Reduce heat to medium; add chopped onion and carrot and cook, stirring frequently, until onion softens, about 2 minutes. Stir in garlic and cook 1 minute. Add wine, tomato paste, and bay leaf; heat to boiling, stirring to blend in tomato paste. Pour wine mixture and broth over chicken. Cover slow cooker and cook on Low 8 hours or on High 4 hours.

5 To serve, discard bay leaf. With large spoon, transfer chicken and sauce to deep platter; sprinkle with bacon.

EACH SERVING: ABOUT 400 CALORIES | 52G PROTEIN | 20G CARBOHYDRATE | 13G TOTAL FAT (4G SATURATED) | 5G FIBER | 156MG CHOLESTEROL | 690MG SODIUM

CHICKEN, BOUILLABAISSE-STYLE

Instead of high-maintenance seafood, this delectable bouillabaisse boasts boneless, skinless chicken thighs simmered in a traditional saffron broth.

ACTIVE TIME: 30 MINUTES · SLOW-COOK TIME: 8 HOURS ON LOW OR 4 HOURS ON HIGH
MAKES: 8 MAIN-DISH SERVINGS

1	TABLESPOON OLIVE OIL	2	GARLIC CLOVES, FINELY CHOPPED
3	POUNDS BONE-IN CHICKEN THIGHS, SKIN AND FAT REMOVED	1¾	CUPS CHICKEN BROTH (TO MAKE HOMEMADE, SEE PAGE 17)
½	TEASPOON SALT	1	CAN (14½ OUNCES) DICED TOMATOES
¼	TEASPOON FRESHLY GROUND BLACK PEPPER	1	BAY LEAF
		½	TEASPOON DRIED THYME
1	LARGE BULB FENNEL (1½ POUNDS)	¼	TEASPOON SAFFRON THREADS, CRUMBLED
½	CUP DRY WHITE WINE		
1	MEDIUM ONION, CHOPPED		CRUSTY FRENCH BREAD (OPTIONAL)

1 In 12-inch skillet, heat oil over medium-high heat until hot. Sprinkle chicken thighs with salt and pepper. Add chicken to skillet in 2 batches and cook, turning once and adding more oil if necessary, until lightly browned on both sides, 7 to 8 minutes per batch. With tongs, transfer chicken to bowl when browned.

2 Meanwhile, trim stems and tough outer layers from fennel bulb. Cut bulb into quarters, then thinly slice crosswise.

3 After chicken is browned, add wine to skillet and heat to boiling, stirring to loosen any browned bits. Boil 1 minute.

4 In 4¼- to 6-quart slow-cooker bowl, combine fennel, onion, garlic, broth, tomatoes with their juice, bay leaf, thyme, and saffron. Top with browned chicken, any juices in bowl, and wine mixture from skillet; do not stir. Cover slow cooker and cook on Low 8 hours or on High 4 hours.

5 With tongs, transfer chicken to serving bowls. Skim and discard fat from sauce and bay leaf. Pour sauce over chicken. Serve with bread, if desired.

EACH SERVING: ABOUT 175 CALORIES | 22G PROTEIN | 9G CARBOHYDRATE | 6G TOTAL FAT (1G SATURATED) | 3G FIBER | 85MG CHOLESTEROL | 580MG SODIUM

BEEF CARBONNADE

A hot and savory pot of beef stew is a great antidote to a dark winter's evening. Serve it over egg noodles for an extra-cozy meal.

ACTIVE TIME: 30 MINUTES · **SLOW-COOK TIME:** 8 HOURS ON LOW
MAKES: 10 MAIN-DISH SERVINGS

2   TABLESPOONS OLIVE OIL

4   POUNDS WELL-TRIMMED BONELESS BEEF CHUCK, CUT INTO 1½-INCH CHUNKS

3   TABLESPOONS ALL-PURPOSE FLOUR

½   TEASPOON SALT

¼   TEASPOON GROUND BLACK PEPPER

1¾ CUPS BEEF BROTH

2   LARGE ONIONS (12 OUNCES EACH), EACH CUT IN HALF AND THINLY SLICED

1   CLOVE GARLIC, CRUSHED WITH SIDE OF CHEF'S KNIFE

12 OUNCES DARK BEER

½   TEASPOON DRIED THYME

1   PACKAGE (16 OUNCES) MEDIUM EGG NOODLES

½   CUP LOOSELY PACKED FRESH PARSLEY LEAVES, CHOPPED

1   In 12-inch skillet, heat oil over medium-high until very hot. In large bowl, combine beef chunks, flour, salt, and pepper; toss to coat beef evenly. Add beef chunks to skillet in three batches, and cook 5 to 6 minutes per batch or until well browned on all sides, stirring occasionally and adding more oil if necessary. With slotted spoon, transfer beef to medium bowl once it is browned.

2   After all beef is browned, add broth to skillet and heat to boiling over high heat, stirring to loosen any browned bits. Boil 1 minute, stirring.

3   Meanwhile, in 6- to 6½-quart slow-cooker bowl, stir together onions, garlic, beer, and thyme. Top with browned beef and any juices, plus broth mixture from skillet; do not stir. Cover slow cooker with lid, and cook as manufacturer directs on Low for 8 hours.

4   About 20 minutes before beef mixture is done, prepare noodles as label directs. Skim and discard any fat from cooking liquid in slow-cooker bowl.

5   To serve, divide noodles evenly among serving bowls; spoon beef mixture and sauce over noodles, then sprinkle with chopped parsley.

EACH SERVING: ABOUT 505 CALORIES | 48G PROTEIN | 41G CARBOHYDRATE | 15G TOTAL FAT (4G SATURATED) | 3G FIBER | 129MG CHOLESTEROL | 380MG SODIUM

LATIN-STYLE BEEF

Ropa vieja, the Spanish name for this Latin-style braised beef literally means "old clothes," because the meat is cooked until it's so tender it can be shredded into what resembles a pile of rags.

ACTIVE TIME: 15 MINUTES · **SLOW-COOK TIME:** 9 HOURS ON LOW

MAKES: 10 MAIN-DISH SERVINGS

½ CUP DRAINED SLICED PICKLED JALAPEÑO CHILES

3 RED, ORANGE, AND/OR YELLOW PEPPERS, CUT INTO ¼-INCH-WIDE SLICES

2 GARLIC CLOVES, THINLY SLICED

1 LARGE ONION (12 OUNCES), CUT IN HALF AND SLICED

1 TEASPOON GROUND CUMIN

½ TEASPOON DRIED OREGANO

1 BAY LEAF

1 TEASPOON SALT

2 BEEF FLANK STEAKS (3½ POUNDS TOTAL)

1 CAN (14½ OUNCES) WHOLE TOMATOES IN JUICE

WARM TORTILLAS (OPTIONAL)

1 In 6- to 6½-quart slow-cooker bowl, stir together jalapeños, peppers, garlic, onion, cumin, oregano, bay leaf, and salt. Top with flank steaks, cutting steaks if necessary to fit into slow-cooker bowl. Using kitchen shears, coarsely cut up tomatoes in can. Pour tomatoes with their juice over steaks; do not stir. Cover slow cooker and cook on Low for 9 hours.

2 Using a slotted spoon, transfer steaks with vegetables to large bowl. Discard bay leaf. Using 2 forks, shred steaks, with the grain, into fine strips. Skim and discard fat from cooking liquid in slow-cooker bowl. Stir cooking liquid into steak mixture. Spoon into serving bowls and serve with tortillas, if desired.

EACH SERVING: ABOUT 300 CALORIES | 36G PROTEIN | 8G CARBOHYDRATE | 13G TOTAL FAT (5G SATURATED) | 2G FIBER | 66MG CHOLESTEROL | 455MG SODIUM

LAMB AND ROOT VEGETABLE TAGINE

We included dried apricots, leg of lamb, and heaps of root vegetables in this tender slow-cooker stew. For photo, see page 32.

ACTIVE TIME: 30 MINUTES · **SLOW-COOK TIME:** 8 HOURS ON LOW
MAKES: 10 MAIN-DISH SERVINGS

1 TABLESPOON VEGETABLE OIL	1 POUND PARSNIPS (6 MEDIUM), PEELED AND CUT INTO 1-INCH PIECES
4 POUNDS WELL-TRIMMED LEG OF LAMB, DEBONED, CUT INTO 1-INCH PIECES	½ CUP DRIED APRICOTS, EACH CUT IN HALF
½ TEASPOON SALT	2 TEASPOONS GROUND CORIANDER
1¾ CUPS CHICKEN BROTH (TO MAKE HOMEMADE, SEE PAGE 17)	2 TEASPOONS GROUND CUMIN
1 MEDIUM ONION, CHOPPED	½ TEASPOON GROUND CINNAMON
2 GARLIC CLOVES, THINLY SLICED	2 CUPS PLAIN COUSCOUS
1 POUND SWEET POTATOES (2 MEDIUM), PEELED AND CUT INTO 1-INCH PIECES	¾ CUP PITTED GREEN OLIVES, CHOPPED
	FRESH CILANTRO LEAVES FOR GARNISH

1 In 12-inch skillet, heat oil over medium-high heat until very hot. Sprinkle lamb with salt. Add lamb to skillet in 3 batches and cook, stirring occasionally and adding more oil if necessary, until lamb is browned on all sides, 5 to 6 minutes per batch. With slotted spoon, transfer lamb to medium bowl when browned.

2 After lamb is browned, add broth to skillet and heat to boiling over high heat, stirring to loosen browned bits. Boil 1 minute.

3 Meanwhile, in 6- to 6½-quart slow-cooker bowl, combine onion, garlic, sweet potatoes, parsnips, apricots, coriander, cumin, and cinnamon. Top with lamb, any juices in bowl, and broth mixture; do not stir. Cover slow cooker and cook on Low for 8 hours.

4 After lamb has cooked, prepare couscous as label directs.

5 Skim and discard fat from cooking liquid. Reserve ¼ cup chopped olives; stir remaining olives into lamb mixture.

6 Spoon lamb mixture over couscous in bowls. Sprinkle with reserved chopped olives. Garnish with cilantro.

EACH SERVING: ABOUT 475 CALORIES | 44G PROTEIN | 50G CARBOHYDRATE | 11G TOTAL FAT (3G SATURATED) | 6G FIBER | 116MG CHOLESTEROL | 600MG SODIUM

SIMMERING PORK SHOULDER

Pork cooked in a slow cooker becomes so tender it almost melts in your mouth. This fragrant, Asian-style stew is simmered for hours in a combination of soy sauce, dry sherry, fresh ginger, and orange peel.

ACTIVE TIME: 30 MINUTES · **SLOW-COOK TIME:** 8 HOURS ON LOW
MAKES: 10 MAIN-DISH SERVINGS

¼   CUP PACKED BROWN SUGAR

¼   CUP DRY SHERRY

¼   CUP SEASONED RICE VINEGAR

¼   CUP PLUS 1 TABLESPOON REDUCED-SODIUM SOY SAUCE

1   MEDIUM ONION, CHOPPED

1   PIECE (2 INCHES) FRESH GINGER, PEELED AND THINLY SLICED INTO ROUNDS

2   GARLIC CLOVES, CRUSHED WITH GARLIC PRESS

2   STRIPS (3" BY ¾" EACH) ORANGE PEEL

1   CINNAMON STICK (3 INCHES)

1   WHOLE STAR ANISE

1   POUND PEELED BABY CARROTS

4   POUNDS WELL-TRIMMED BONELESS PORK SHOULDER, CUT INTO 1½-INCH PIECES (SEE TIP)

2   BAGS (10 OUNCES EACH) FROZEN BROCCOLI FLORETS, THAWED

1   In 6- to 6½-quart slow-cooker bowl, combine brown sugar, sherry, vinegar, and ¼ cup soy sauce. Stir in onion, ginger, garlic, orange peel, cinnamon, star anise, and carrots. Top with pork; do not stir. Cover slow cooker and cook on Low for 8 hours.

2   When pork has cooked 8 hours, uncover and stir in broccoli. Cover and cook until broccoli is heated through, about 10 minutes.

3   Discard cinnamon and star anise. Skim and discard fat from cooking liquid. Stir in remaining 1 tablespoon soy sauce.

TIP If the pork isn't well trimmed when you buy it, purchase 5 pounds and cut away the excess fat and skin to yield 4 pounds of solid meat.

EACH SERVING: ABOUT 335 CALORIES | 38G PROTEIN | 16G CARBOHYDRATE | 13G TOTAL FAT (4G SATURATED) | 2G FIBER | 121MG CHOLESTEROL | 645MG SODIUM

LENTIL STEW WITH BUTTERNUT SQUASH

Rich in vitamins A and C, butternut squash adds a subtle sweetness to this hearty lentil stew.

ACTIVE TIME: 20 MINUTES · **SLOW-COOK TIME:** 8 HOURS ON LOW
MAKES: 8 MAIN-DISH SERVINGS

- 3 LARGE STALKS CELERY, CUT INTO ¼-INCH SLICES
- 1 LARGE ONION (12 OUNCES), CHOPPED
- 1 LARGE BUTTERNUT SQUASH (2½ POUNDS), PEELED, SEEDED, AND CUT INTO 1-INCH PIECES
- 1 POUND BROWN LENTILS
- 4 CUPS WATER
- 1¾ CUPS VEGETABLE BROTH (TO MAKE HOMEMADE, SEE PAGE 16)
- ½ TEASPOON DRIED ROSEMARY
- ¾ TEASPOON SALT
- ¼ TEASPOON GROUND BLACK PEPPER
- 1 OUNCE PARMESAN OR PECORINO-ROMANO CHEESE, SHAVED WITH VEGETABLE PEELER
- ¼ CUP LOOSELY PACKED FRESH PARSLEY LEAVES, CHOPPED

1 In 4½- to 6-quart slow-cooker bowl, combine celery, onion, squash, lentils, water, broth, rosemary, salt, and pepper. Cover slow cooker and cook on Low 8 hours.

2 To serve, spoon stew into serving bowls; top with Parmesan and sprinkle with parsley.

EACH SERVING: ABOUT 285 CALORIES | 20G PROTEIN | 51G CARBOHYDRATE | 2G TOTAL FAT (1G SATURATED) | 20G FIBER | 3MG CHOLESTEROL | 420MG SODIUM

VEGETARIAN LASAGNA

This lasagna lets you enjoy the great taste without all the work—thanks to no-boil noodles, prepared sauce, frozen spinach, and shredded cheese.

ACTIVE TIME: 15 MINUTES · **SLOW-COOK TIME:** 2½ HOURS ON LOW OR 1½ HOURS ON HIGH

MAKES: 8 MAIN-DISH SERVINGS

1   JAR (25 TO 26 OUNCES) MARINARA SAUCE

1   CAN (14½ OUNCES) DICED TOMATOES

1   PACKAGE (8 TO 9 OUNCES) OVEN-READY (NO-BOIL) LASAGNA NOODLES

1   CONTAINER (15 OUNCES) PART-SKIM RICOTTA CHEESE

1   PACKAGE (8 OUNCES) SHREDDED ITALIAN CHEESE BLEND OR SHREDDED MOZZARELLA CHEESE

1   PACKAGE (10 OUNCES) FROZEN CHOPPED SPINACH, THAWED AND SQUEEZED DRY

1   CUP FROZEN VEGGIE CRUMBLES (SEE TIP; OPTIONAL)

FRESHLY GRATED PARMESAN CHEESE (OPTIONAL)

1   In medium bowl, combine marinara and tomatoes with their juice.

2   Spray 4½- to 6-quart slow-cooker bowl with nonstick cooking spray. Spoon 1 cup tomato-sauce mixture into bowl. Arrange one-quarter of noodles over sauce, overlapping noodles and breaking into large pieces to cover as much sauce as possible. Spoon about ¾ cup sauce over noodles, then top with one third of ricotta (about ½ cup), and ½ cup shredded cheese. Spread half of spinach (or one third if not using veggie crumbles) over cheese.

3   Repeat layering two more times beginning with noodles, but in middle layer, replace spinach with frozen veggie crumbles, if using. Place the remaining noodles over spinach, then top with remaining sauce and shredded cheese.

4   Cover slow cooker and cook on Low 2½ to 3 hours or on High 1½ to 1¾ hours or until cheese is melted and noodles are very tender. Sprinkle Parmesan on top of lasagna, if desired. Use spatula to cut and serve.

TIP   Frozen veggie crumbles are a heat-and-serve vegetarian meat alternative found in your grocer's freezer; you can substitute 8 ounces ground beef, browned, if you prefer.

EACH SERVING: ABOUT 415 CALORIES | 24G PROTEIN | 41G CARBOHYDRATE | 17G TOTAL FAT (8G SATURATED) | 6G FIBER | 37MG CHOLESTEROL | 1,120MG SODIUM

PERFECT PASTAS

Oodles of noodles, whether cheesy or blanketed in sauce, are the ultimate comfort food. From a light and luscious penne tossed with seasonal vegetables and a dollop of pesto to spaghetti carbonara, a restaurant favorite featuring a creamy, bacon-specked sauce, these dishes are sure to satisfy.

We offer two kinds of colorful pasta primavera (one with chicken breast, the other shrimp); both make ideal company fare. But if you crave meat sauce, dig into our hearty lasagna toss or sausage baked ziti. And, of course, we haven't forgotten the mac and cheese: our version, made with two kinds of cheese and a light and crispy bread-crumb topping, is irresistible.

Chicken Bolognese (recipe on page 58)

EASY TOMATO SAUCE

Sometimes all you want is a **warm bowl of pasta tossed with tomato sauce**. Here's a simple recipe, plus four delicious variations. Pair with one pound cooked pasta of choice to make four main-dish servings.

ACTIVE TIME: 5 MINUTES · **TOTAL TIME:** 16 MINUTES
MAKES: 4 SERVINGS

- 4 TABLESPOONS OLIVE OIL
- 4 CLOVES GARLIC, CRUSHED WITH GARLIC PRESS
- 4 POUNDS RIPE TOMATOES (ABOUT 6 MEDIUM), COARSELY CHOPPED
- ¼ TEASPOON SALT
- ⅛ TEASPOON GROUND BLACK PEPPER

In 12-inch skillet, heat oil over medium-high until hot. Add garlic; cook 1 minute or until golden, stirring. Add tomatoes, salt, and pepper and cook, uncovered, 10 minutes or until lightly thickened. Remove skillet from heat.

EACH ½ CUP: ABOUT 85 CALORIES | 2G PROTEIN | 8G CARBOHYDRATE | 6G TOTAL FAT (1G SATURATED) | 2G FIBER | 0MG CHOLESTEROL | 130MG SODIUM

CHIPOTLE TOMATO SAUCE

Prepare Easy Tomato Sauce as directed, but add **½ teaspoon ground chipotle chili pepper** along with the garlic.

BASIL OR ROSEMARY TOMATO SAUCE

Prepare Easy Tomato Sauce as directed, but after removing sauce from heat, stir in **¼ cup loosely packed fresh basil leaves, chopped,** or **1 teaspoon chopped fresh rosemary**.

SAGE TOMATO SAUCE

Prepare Easy Tomato Sauce as directed, but after removing sauce from heat, stir in **1 tablespoon butter or margarine, plus 1 teaspoon chopped fresh sage**.

FARFALLE WITH GRILLED VEGETABLES

A medley of grilled veggies makes pasta extra good. If you have fresh basil, mint, parsley, or dill in the garden or the fridge, chop ¼ cup and stir it into this already colorful dish just before serving.

ACTIVE TIME: 20 MINUTES · TOTAL TIME: 55 MINUTES
MAKES: 4 MAIN-DISH SERVINGS

- 2 MEDIUM RED PEPPERS, EACH CUT LENGTHWISE INTO QUARTERS, SEEDS AND STEMS DISCARDED
- 2 MEDIUM ZUCCHINI AND/OR SUMMER SQUASH (8 OUNCES EACH), CUT INTO ½-INCH-THICK SLICES
- 1 MEDIUM ONION, CUT INTO ½-INCH-THICK ROUND SLICES
- 2 TABLESPOONS OLIVE OIL
- ¼ TEASPOON SALT
- ¼ TEASPOON GROUND BLACK PEPPER
- 1 PACKAGE (16 OUNCES) FARFALLE
- 2 LARGE TOMATOES, CHOPPED
- ⅓ CUP FRESHLY GRATED PECORINO-ROMANO CHEESE, PLUS ADDITIONAL FOR SERVING

1 Heat large covered saucepot of *salted water* to boiling over high heat.
2 Meanwhile, preheat outdoor grill for direct grilling over medium heat. Place red peppers, zucchini, and onion in large bowl; add oil, salt, and black pepper. Toss until vegetables are evenly coated.
3 Place vegetables on hot grill grate; cover and cook 10 to 12 minutes or until vegetables are tender and lightly charred, turning once. While vegetables are grilling, add pasta to boiling water and cook as label directs. As vegetables are done grilling, transfer to cutting board and coarsely chop.
4 Reserve ¼ *cup pasta cooking water*. Drain pasta. Return pasta and reserved cooking water to saucepot; stir in tomatoes, grilled vegetables, and ⅓ cup Pecorino. Serve with additional Pecorino.

EACH SERVING: ABOUT 575 CALORIES | 20G PROTEIN | 100G CARBOHYDRATE | 11G TOTAL FAT (2G SATURATED) | 7G FIBER | 7MG CHOLESTEROL | 385MG SODIUM

PENNE GENOVESE WITH WHITE BEANS AND PESTO

An onion-flecked white bean sauté adds heft to this fresh and healthy pesto pasta dish, making it light yet satisfying.

ACTIVE TIME: 20 MINUTES · TOTAL TIME: 50 MINUTES
MAKES: 6 MAIN-DISH SERVINGS

- 12 OUNCES WHOLE-WHEAT PENNE OR ROTINI
- 1½ CUPS PACKED FRESH BASIL LEAVES
- 1 GARLIC CLOVE
- 3 TABLESPOONS WATER
- 3 TABLESPOONS EXTRA-VIRGIN OLIVE OIL
- ¼ TEASPOON SALT
- ½ TEASPOON GROUND BLACK PEPPER
- ½ CUP FRESHLY GRATED PARMESAN CHEESE
- 1 SMALL ONION (4 TO 6 OUNCES), CHOPPED
- 1 CAN (15 OUNCES) WHITE KIDNEY BEANS (CANNELLINI), RINSED AND DRAINED
- 1 PINT GRAPE TOMATOES (RED, YELLOW, AND ORANGE MIX IF AVAILABLE), CUT INTO QUARTERS

1   Heat large covered saucepot of *salted water* to boiling over high heat. Add pasta and cook as label directs.

2   Meanwhile, make pesto: In food processor with knife blade attached, blend basil, garlic, water, 2 tablespoons oil, salt, and pepper until pureed, stopping processor occasionally and scraping bowl with rubber spatula. Add Parmesan; pulse to combine. Set aside.

3   In 12-inch skillet, heat remaining 1 tablespoon oil over medium heat until very hot; add onion and cook 5 to 7 minutes or until beginning to soften. Stir in beans and cook 5 minutes longer, stirring occasionally.

4   Reserve ¼ *cup pasta cooking water.* Drain pasta and return to saucepot; stir in bean mixture, pesto, tomatoes, and reserved cooking water. Toss.

EACH SERVING: ABOUT 375 CALORIES | 15G PROTEIN | 59G CARBOHYDRATE | 10G TOTAL FAT (2G SATURATED) | 9G FIBER | 5MG CHOLESTEROL | 435MG SODIUM

LASAGNA TOSS BOLOGNESE

If only lasagna, that perennial family favorite didn't take two and a half hours to prepare and bake! Luckily our streamlined version clocks in at just thirty minutes from saucepot to pasta bowl, without losing any of the rich flavors of the original.

ACTIVE TIME: 15 MINUTES · TOTAL TIME: 45 MINUTES
MAKES: 6 MAIN-DISH SERVINGS

---

1 PACKAGE (16 OUNCES) LASAGNA NOODLES (SEE TIP)

2 TEASPOONS OLIVE OIL

1 POUND LEAN GROUND BEEF OR MEATLOAF MIX (GROUND BEEF, PORK, AND VEAL)

½ CUP DRY RED WINE

1 JAR (24 OUNCES) MARINARA SAUCE

⅓ CUP WHOLE MILK

¾ CUP PART-SKIM RICOTTA CHEESE

½ CUP FRESH BASIL LEAVES, CHOPPED

¼ CUP FRESHLY GRATED PECORINO-ROMANO CHEESE

¼ TEASPOON GROUND BLACK PEPPER

⅓ CUP SHREDDED PART-SKIM MOZZARELLA CHEESE

1 Heat large covered saucepot of *salted water* to boiling over high heat. Add lasagna noodles and cook as label directs or until al dente.

2 Meanwhile, in 12-inch skillet, heat oil over medium-high heat until hot. Add meat and cook, breaking it up with spoon, until no longer pink, about 3 minutes. (If using meatloaf mix, drain off fat.) Add wine; cook 2 to 3 minutes or until almost evaporated. Stir in marinara sauce, then heat to boiling. Simmer over low heat 5 minutes, stirring occasionally. Stir in milk; simmer 5 minutes.

3 In bowl, stir ricotta with basil, Pecorino, and pepper; set aside.

4 Drain noodles and return to saucepot. Add meat sauce and mozzarella; toss well.

5 Spoon onto 6 warm plates; top with dollops of ricotta mixture.

TIP Don't be tempted to use no-boil lasagna noodles to save time with this recipe—the noodles will break apart when tossed.

EACH SERVING: ABOUT 655 CALORIES | 32G PROTEIN | 71G CARBOHYDRATE | 26G TOTAL FAT (10G SATURATED) | 4G FIBER | 71MG CHOLESTEROL | 800MG SODIUM

CHICKEN BOLOGNESE

This tasty recipe combines linguine, lean ground chicken, and classic Bolognese ingredients for a family dinner that everyone will love. For photo, see page 50.

ACTIVE TIME: 25 MINUTES · TOTAL TIME: 1 HOUR 5 MINUTES
MAKES: 6 MAIN-DISH SERVINGS

- 12 OUNCES LINGUINE OR FETTUCINE
- 4 TEASPOONS OLIVE OIL
- 1 POUND GROUND CHICKEN BREAST
- ½ TEASPOON SALT
- ¼ TEASPOON GROUND BLACK PEPPER
- 2 MEDIUM CARROTS, PEELED AND CHOPPED
- 2 MEDIUM STALKS CELERY, CHOPPED
- 1 LARGE ONION (12 OUNCES), CHOPPED

- 1 GARLIC CLOVE, CRUSHED WITH GARLIC PRESS
- 1 CAN (28 OUNCES) CRUSHED TOMATOES
- ½ CUP REDUCED-FAT MILK (2%)
- ⅓ CUP FRESHLY GRATED PARMESAN CHEESE
- ¼ CUP LOOSELY PACKED FRESH PARSLEY LEAVES, CHOPPED

1 Heat large covered saucepot of *salted water* to boiling over high heat. Add pasta and cook as label directs.

2 While pasta cooks, in nonstick 12-inch skillet, heat 2 teaspoons oil over medium heat for 1 minute. Add ground chicken to skillet; sprinkle with ¼ teaspoon salt. Cook chicken, stirring occasionally, until no longer pink, 8 to 9 minutes. Transfer chicken along with any juices in skillet to medium bowl; set aside.

3 To same skillet, add remaining 2 teaspoons oil, carrots, celery, onion, and garlic; cook, stirring occasionally, until vegetables are lightly browned and tender, 10 to 12 minutes. Stir in tomatoes, remaining ¼ teaspoon salt, and pepper; heat to boiling. Reduce heat to medium-low and simmer, uncovered, 10 minutes, stirring occasionally.

4 Stir in chicken and milk; heat through.

5 Reserve ¼ *cup pasta cooking water*. Drain pasta and return to saucepot; stir in sauce from skillet, Parmesan, parsley, and reserved cooking water and toss to coat pasta.

EACH SERVING: ABOUT 410 CALORIES | 29G PROTEIN | 59G CARBOHYDRATE | 6G TOTAL FAT (2G SATURATED) | 5G FIBER | 49MG CHOLESTEROL | 800MG SODIUM

SPAGHETTI CARBONARA

Here's a restaurant favorite you can make at home with ease. Beaten eggs and plenty of Romano cheese form a light, creamy sauce in this bacon-studded pasta dish.

ACTIVE TIME: 10 MINUTES · **TOTAL TIME:** 45 MINUTES
MAKES: 4 MAIN-DISH SERVINGS

1   PACKAGE (16 OUNCES) SPAGHETTI

1   TABLESPOON OLIVE OIL

3   THICK SLICES BACON OR 4 OUNCES PANCETTA, CUT INTO ¼-INCH PIECES

1   SMALL ONION, CHOPPED

5   LARGE EGGS

½   CUP FRESHLY GRATED PECORINO-ROMANO CHEESE, PLUS ADDITIONAL FOR SERVING

¼   TEASPOON GROUND BLACK PEPPER, PLUS COARSELY GROUND BLACK PEPPER

¼   CUP LOOSELY PACKED FRESH PARSLEY LEAVES, CHOPPED

1   Heat large covered saucepot of *salted water* to boiling over high heat. Add spaghetti and cook as label directs.

2   Meanwhile, in nonstick 12-inch skillet, heat oil over medium heat 1 minute. Add bacon and cook until browned. With slotted spoon, transfer bacon to paper-towel-lined plate. Pour off all but 2 tablespoons fat from skillet; add onion and cook 5 to 6 minutes or until tender. Remove skillet from heat.

3   Reserve *¼ cup pasta cooking water.* Drain pasta; add to skillet with reserved water and bacon. Cook over medium heat, stirring, until water is absorbed. In bowl, whisk eggs with Romano and pepper.

4   Remove skillet from heat; stir in egg mixture (heat from pasta will cook eggs). Add parsley and toss until pasta is well coated. Spoon into warm pasta bowl; serve with Romano and coarsely ground pepper to taste.

EACH SERVING: ABOUT 695 CALORIES | 29G PROTEIN | 88G CARBOHYDRATE | 24G TOTAL FAT (8G SATURATED) | 3G FIBER | 290MG CHOLESTEROL | 590MG SODIUM

CHICKEN PASTA PRIMAVERA

Thanks to the addictively rich cream sauce, your family will clamor for seconds, while you'll appreciate the abundant veggies they're getting.

ACTIVE TIME: 25 MINUTES · **TOTAL TIME:** 55 MINUTES
MAKES: 6 MAIN-DISH SERVINGS

12 OUNCES FUSILLI OR CAVATAPPI

2 GREEN ONIONS

4 TEASPOONS OLIVE OIL

1½ POUNDS SKINLESS, BONELESS CHICKEN-BREAST HALVES, CUT INTO 1-INCH PIECES

½ TEASPOON SALT

¼ TEASPOON GROUND BLACK PEPPER

1 GARLIC CLOVE, CRUSHED WITH GARLIC PRESS

1 POUND ASPARAGUS, TRIMMED AND CUT INTO 1-INCH PIECES

1 MEDIUM RED PEPPER, THINLY SLICED

½ CUP HEAVY OR WHIPPING CREAM

¼ TEASPOON CRUSHED RED PEPPER

½ CUP FRESHLY GRATED PARMESAN CHEESE

¼ CUP LOOSELY PACKED FRESH BASIL LEAVES, THINLY SLICED

1 Heat large covered saucepot of *salted water* to boiling over high heat. Add pasta and cook as label directs. Drain pasta, reserving *½ cup cooking water*. Return pasta and reserved cooking water to saucepot.

2 Meanwhile, slice green onions and reserve 2 tablespoons dark-green tops for garnish. In 12-inch skillet, heat 2 teaspoons oil over medium-high heat until hot. Sprinkle chicken with ¼ teaspoon each salt and black pepper. Add chicken to skillet and cook, stirring occasionally, until chicken is browned and no longer pink throughout, 6 to 7 minutes. Transfer to medium bowl; set aside.

3 To skillet, add remaining 2 teaspoons oil; reduce heat to medium. Add green onions and garlic; cook 1 minute, stirring. Add asparagus and red pepper; cook, stirring frequently, until vegetables are tender-crisp, 6 to 7 minutes. Stir in cream, crushed red pepper, and remaining ¼ teaspoon salt. Heat to boiling over medium-high heat. Stir in chicken and remove skillet from heat.

4 To saucepot with pasta and reserved cooking water, add Parmesan, chicken mixture, and basil; stir to combine. Spoon into bowls; garnish with reserved green onion.

EACH SERVING: ABOUT 485 CALORIES | 38G PROTEIN | 46G CARBOHYDRATE | 15G TOTAL FAT (7G SATURATED) | 3G FIBER | 98MG CHOLESTEROL | 470MG SODIUM

SHRIMP PASTA PRIMAVERA

This colorful pasta is a great recipe to whip up for guests. Serve with a salad of baby greens and some crusty Italian bread.

ACTIVE TIME: 15 MINUTES · TOTAL TIME: 50 MINUTES
MAKES: 6 MAIN-DISH SERVINGS

16 OUNCES (1 PACKAGE) MEDIUM SHELL OR BOW-TIE PASTA

4 MEDIUM CARROTS, SLICED DIAGONALLY INTO ⅛-INCH-THICK SLICES

2 CUPS BROCCOLI FLORETS (HALF-OUNCE BAG) AND/OR 2 CUPS 2-INCH PIECES ASPARAGUS (8 OUNCES)

6 OUNCES SNAP PEAS OR SNOW PEAS, STRINGS REMOVED, OR 1 CUP FROZEN PEAS

1 CUP HEAVY OR WHIPPING CREAM

1 TEASPOON GRATED FRESH LEMON PEEL

1 TEASPOON SALT

½ TEASPOON GROUND BLACK PEPPER

1 POUND UNCOOKED FROZEN OR FRESH SHELLED AND DEVEINED LARGE SHRIMP, WITH TAIL PART OF SHELL LEFT ON, IF YOU LIKE

3 PLUM TOMATOES OR 2 MEDIUM TOMATOES, COARSELY CHOPPED

1 CUP LOOSELY PACKED MIXED FRESH HERBS, SUCH AS BASIL, MINT, DILL, AND/OR PARSLEY LEAVES, COARSELY CHOPPED

1 Heat large covered saucepot of *salted water* to boiling over high heat.

2 Add pasta to water in saucepot; heat to boiling over high heat and cook 3 minutes. Add carrots, broccoli, and snap peas to pasta; heat to boiling and cook 3 minutes longer. Remove ½ *cup pasta cooking water;* set aside. Drain pasta and vegetables in colander when pasta is tender yet still slightly firm (al dente); set aside.

3 In same saucepot, heat cream, lemon peel, reserved pasta cooking water, salt, and black pepper to boiling over high heat, stirring occasionally. Add frozen shrimp and cook 5 minutes or just until shrimp turn opaque throughout. (If using fresh shrimp, cook only 2 to 3 minutes.)

4 Add pasta and vegetables to shrimp mixture in saucepot. Add tomatoes and mixed herbs and toss to combine; heat through and serve.

EACH SERVING: ABOUT 545 CALORIES | 28G PROTEIN | 69G CARBOHYDRATE | 18G TOTAL FAT (10G SATURATED FAT) | 6G FIBER | 170MG CHOLESTEROL | 650MG SODIUM

SAUSAGE AND PEPPER BAKED ZITI

This yummy new twist on baked ziti will please kids as well as adults. Assemble it up to a day ahead, refrigerate, and bake just before serving.

ACTIVE TIME: 20 MINUTES · **TOTAL TIME:** 1 HOUR 25 MINUTES

MAKES: 2 CASSEROLES, 4 MAIN-DISH SERVINGS EACH

- 1 POUND SWEET AND/OR HOT ITALIAN SAUSAGE LINKS, CASINGS REMOVED
- 4 GARLIC CLOVES, CRUSHED WITH GARLIC PRESS
- 2 LARGE RED, GREEN, AND/OR YELLOW PEPPERS, CUT INTO ¼-INCH SLICES
- 1 JUMBO ONION (1 POUND), CUT IN HALF, THEN CUT CROSSWISE INTO ¼-INCH SLICES
- 1 POUND SLICED WHITE MUSHROOMS
- 1 CAN (28 OUNCES) WHOLE TOMATOES IN PUREE
- 1 CAN (15 OUNCES) TOMATO PUREE
- 1 TEASPOON SALT
- 1 PACKAGE (16 OUNCES) ZITI OR PENNE
- 1 PACKAGE (8 OUNCES) SHREDDED PART-SKIM MOZZARELLA CHEESE
- ½ CUP FRESHLY GRATED PECORINO-ROMANO CHEESE

1 In deep nonstick 12-inch skillet, cook sausage over medium heat 10 minutes or until browned, stirring and breaking it up with side of spoon. With slotted spoon, transfer sausage to medium bowl.

2 In drippings in skillet, cook garlic, peppers, onion, and mushrooms, covered, 10 minutes. Uncover and cook 8 minutes longer or until vegetables are tender and most of liquid has evaporated. Stir in tomatoes and puree, tomato puree, and salt; heat to boiling over medium-high heat, stirring and breaking up tomatoes with side of spoon. Reduce heat to medium-low; cover and cook 10 minutes, stirring occasionally.

3 Meanwhile, heat large covered saucepot of *salted water* to boiling over high heat. Add pasta and cook 2 minutes less than label directs.

4 Preheat oven to 400°F. Reserve ½ *cup pasta cooking water*. Drain pasta. Return pasta and reserved cooking water to saucepot; stir in tomato sauce. Add mozzarella and reserved sausage; toss to combine. Divide mixture evenly between 2 ungreased 2½-quart baking dishes. Sprinkle with Pecorino.

5 Bake 20 to 25 minutes or until tops brown and sauce is bubbling (add 10 minutes if casserole was refrigerated). Let stand 10 minutes before serving.

EACH SERVING: ABOUT 575 CALORIES | 28G PROTEIN | 63G CARBOHYDRATE | 24G TOTAL FAT (10G SATURATED) | 6G FIBER | 62MG CHOLESTEROL | 1,410MG SODIUM

MACARONI AND CHEESE

Oodles of noodles baked in cheese sauce. If there's anything more delicious and comforting than that, we haven't tasted it!

ACTIVE TIME: 15 MINUTES · TOTAL TIME: 45 MINUTES
MAKES: 6 MAIN-DISH SERVINGS

1   PACKAGE (16 OUNCES) FUSILLI

6   CUPS LOW-FAT MILK (1%)

3   TABLESPOONS CORNSTARCH

1   TEASPOON DRY MUSTARD

¾   TEASPOON SALT

⅛   TEASPOON GROUND NUTMEG

½   CUP FRESHLY GRATED PECORINO-ROMANO CHEESE

3   CUPS SHREDDED EXTRA-SHARP CHEDDAR CHEESE

¼   CUP PANKO (JAPANESE-STYLE BREAD CRUMBS)

1   TABLESPOON BUTTER, MELTED

1   Preheat oven to 400°F. Prepare pasta according to package directions.

2   Meanwhile, in large glass bowl, heat milk in microwave on High 2 minutes. To 4-quart saucepan, add milk. Whisk in cornstarch, mustard, salt, and nutmeg until well blended. Cook over medium heat, whisking frequently, until mixture thickens slightly and boils, 8 to 10 minutes. Cook 1 minute longer, whisking constantly. Remove from heat. Stir in Pecorino and then 2½ cups Cheddar until cheese melts.

3   In large mixing bowl, combine pasta and cheese sauce until well mixed. Spoon into shallow 3½-quart baking dish. Combine panko and butter and mix well. Stir in remaining cheese until well combined. Sprinkle over top of pasta and cheese. Bake, uncovered, 25 minutes or until hot and bubbling and bread crumbs are golden brown.

EACH SERVING: ABOUT 700 CALORIES | 37G PROTEIN | 76G CARBOHYDRATE | 28G TOTAL FAT (17G SATURATED) | 2G FIBER | 87MG CHOLESTEROL | 945MG SODIUM

SPAGHETTI PIE WITH PROSCIUTTO AND PEAS

Make this easy pie with freshly cooked spaghetti or use leftover noodles. A garnish of fried, thinly sliced green onions completes the picture.

ACTIVE TIME: 25 MINUTES · **TOTAL TIME:** 40 MINUTES
MAKES: 6 MAIN-DISH SERVINGS

8	OUNCES THICK SPAGHETTI	½	TEASPOON GROUND BLACK PEPPER
4	LARGE EGGS	1	TABLESPOON BUTTER OR MARGARINE
2	LARGE EGG WHITES	1	BUNCH GREEN ONIONS, CUT INTO
1	CONTAINER (15 OUNCES) PART-SKIM RICOTTA CHEESE		¼-INCH PIECES (ABOUT 1 CUP)
		1	CUP FROZEN PEAS
¾	CUP REDUCED-FAT MILK (2%)	6	THIN SLICES PROSCIUTTO (ABOUT 3 OUNCES)
⅛	TEASPOON GROUND NUTMEG		
¼	TEASPOON SALT		

1 Preheat oven to 350°F. Heat large covered saucepot of *salted water* to boiling over high heat. Add spaghetti and cook 2 minutes less than label directs.

2 Meanwhile, in medium bowl, whisk eggs, egg whites, ricotta, milk, nutmeg, salt, and pepper until blended. Set aside. In nonstick 12-inch skillet with oven-safe handle, melt butter over medium heat. Add green onions and cook about 5 minutes or until softened. Remove skillet from heat.

3 Drain spaghetti. To green onions in skillet, add spaghetti and frozen peas; toss to combine. Pour egg mixture over pasta and arrange prosciutto slices on top.

4 Place skillet over medium-high heat and cook egg mixture 3 to 5 minutes or until edges just begin to set. Place skillet in oven and bake 15 minutes or until center is set. Slide pie onto large plate to serve.

EACH SERVING: ABOUT 375 CALORIES | 25G PROTEIN | 38G CARBOHYDRATE | 13G TOTAL FAT (6G SATURATED) | 2G FIBER | 175MG CHOLESTEROL | 700MG SODIUM

COMFORT CLASSICS

Warming and flavorful, these inviting dishes are all chock-full of home-style goodness. We start with a classic roasted chicken paired with a medley of winter vegetables and close with a meat loaf flavored with Cajun seasonings. Either would pair nicely with a selection of our comforting sides, from Potato Gratin with Gruyère (page 111) to Vegetable-Herb Stuffing (page 115).

In between we have hearty casseroles: Choose from pot pies (chicken, vegetable, or chili), a turkey and sweet potato shepherd's pie, enchiladas, and then some. Each is a rich, delicious way to please a crowd. Consider making two and freezing one so you can serve up cozy leftovers on a busy weeknight.

Roasted Chicken with Winter Vegetables (recipe page 70)

ROASTED CHICKEN WITH WINTER VEGETABLES

This no-baste bird, with its crisp, crackly skin is a French classic of comfort and convenience. For photo, see page 68.

ACTIVE TIME: 15 MINUTES · TOTAL TIME: 1 HOURS MAKES: 4 MAIN-DISH SERVINGS

1 LARGE ONION (10 TO 12 OUNCES), CUT INTO ½-INCH-THICK SLICES

1 POUND LARGE BABY RED POTATOES, EACH CUT IN HALF

4 LARGE CARROTS (1 POUND), EACH CUT IN 2-INCH-LONG PIECES

2 SMALL TURNIPS (2 OUNCES EACH), PEELED AND CUT INTO WEDGES

1 SMALL FENNEL BULB (6 OUNCES), TRIMMED, CORED, AND CUT INTO WEDGES

8 FRESH THYME SPRIGS, PLUS ADDITIONAL FOR GARNISH

7 CLOVES GARLIC, CRUSHED WITH SIDE OF KNIFE, PEEL DISCARDED

1 TABLESPOON PLUS 1 TEASPOON OLIVE OIL

½ TEASPOON SALT

⅝ TEASPOON FRESHLY GROUND BLACK PEPPER

1 WHOLE CHICKEN (3 TO 3½ POUNDS)

1 Preheat oven to 450°F. In 18" by 12" jelly-roll pan, arrange onion slices in single layer in center. In large bowl, toss potatoes, carrots, turnips, fennel, 4 thyme sprigs, 3 garlic cloves, 1 tablespoon oil, ¼ teaspoon salt, and ¼ teaspoon pepper until well mixed. Spread in even layer around onion slices in pan.

2 If necessary, remove bag with giblets and neck from chicken cavity; discard or reserve for another use. Rub chicken cavity with remaining ¼ teaspoon salt and ¼ teaspoon pepper. Place remaining 4 thyme sprigs and 4 garlic cloves in cavity and tie legs together with kitchen string. Rub remaining 1 teaspoon oil on chicken and sprinkle with remaining ⅛ teaspoon pepper.

3 Place chicken, breast side up, on onion slices in pan. Roast 45 minutes or until juices run clear when thickest part of thigh is pierced with tip of knife and temperature on meat thermometer inserted into thickest part of thigh reaches 175°F. Let chicken stand in pan 10 minutes to set juices.

4 Meanwhile, transfer vegetables around chicken to serving platter, leaving space in center for chicken. Transfer chicken and onion to serving platter with vegetables, tilting chicken slightly as you lift to allow any juices inside to run into pan. Skim and discard fat from juices in pan; pour into small bowl and serve with chicken. Garnish with additional thyme sprigs.

EACH SERVING: ABOUT 555 CALORIES | 45G PROTEIN | 37G CARBOHYDRATE | 25G TOTAL FAT (6G SATURATED) | 7G FIBER | 160MG CHOLESTEROL | 405MG SODIUM

CHICKEN GUMBO POT PIE

Puff pastry adds an elegant touch to this luscious chicken gumbo.

ACTIVE TIME: 1 HOUR · TOTAL TIME: 1 HOUR 35 MINUTES

MAKES: 2 PIES, 6 MAIN-DISH SERVINGS EACH

- 2 SLICES BACON, CUT INTO ½-INCH PIECES
- 2 POUNDS SKINLESS BONELESS CHICKEN THIGHS, CUT INTO 1-INCH CHUNKS
- 1 TEASPOON SALT
- 2 TABLESPOONS OLIVE OIL
- ¼ CUP ALL-PURPOSE FLOUR
- 1 CUP CHICKEN BROTH (TO MAKE HOMEMADE, SEE PAGE 17)
- 4 MEDIUM STALKS CELERY, SLICED
- 1 JUMBO ONION (ABOUT 1 POUND), CHOPPED
- 1 MEDIUM RED PEPPER, CHOPPED
- 1 TABLESPOON CAJUN SEASONING
- 1 BAG (16 OUNCES) FROZEN SLICED OKRA
- 1 CAN (14 TO 14½ OUNCES) STEWED TOMATOES
- 1 PACKAGE (17.4 OUNCES) FROZEN PUFF PASTRY SHEETS, THAWED

1 In nonstick 12-inch skillet, cook bacon over medium heat 6 to 8 minutes or until browned, stirring occasionally. With slotted spoon, transfer bacon to paper towels to drain. Sprinkle ½ teaspoon salt on chicken. In bacon fat in skillet, cook chicken, in 2 batches, 5 to 6 minutes per batch or until beginning to brown. With tongs, transfer chicken to bowl.

2 In same skillet, heat 2 tablespoons olive oil over medium heat 1 minute. Stir in flour and cook about 7 minutes or until deep golden-brown, stirring constantly. Gradually add in broth, stirring with whisk to prevent lumps; heat to boiling. Boil 1 minute, stirring. Remove skillet from heat.

3 Meanwhile, preheat oven to 400°F. In 5- or 6-quart Dutch oven, heat remaining 1 tablespoon olive oil over medium-high until hot. Add celery, onion, and pepper. Cook about 10 minutes or until all vegetables are tender, stirring occasionally. Stir in Cajun seasoning; cook 30 seconds. Add chicken-broth mixture, okra, stewed tomatoes, and ½ teaspoon salt; heat to boiling over high heat. Stir in chicken and bacon; reduce heat to medium and cook 10 minutes or until chicken is no longer pink inside, stirring occasionally.

4 Divide gumbo between 2 ungreased 9½-inch deep-dish pie plates. Top each with 1 sheet puff pastry, tucking pastry corners under to form a round top. Cut six 1-inch slits in pastry to allow steam to escape during baking.

5 Bake 35 minutes or until pastry is golden-brown and puffed.

EACH SERVING: ABOUT 430 CALORIES | 21G PROTEIN | 29G CARBOHYDRATE | 26G TOTAL FAT (7G SATURATED) | 4G FIBER | 67MG CHOLESTEROL | 690MG SODIUM

TURKEY OR CHICKEN SHORTCAKES

This next-day dish lends leftover poultry rich flavor.

ACTIVE TIME: 25 MINUTES · TOTAL TIME: 1 HOUR
MAKES: 4 MAIN-DISH SERVINGS

2 TEASPOONS BAKING POWDER

1⅓ CUPS PLUS 2 TABLESPOONS ALL-PURPOSE FLOUR

1 TEASPOON SALT

½ TEASPOON GROUND BLACK PEPPER

4 TABLESPOONS BUTTER

1 CUP REDUCED-FAT MILK (2%)

1 SMALL ONION, CHOPPED

3 MEDIUM CARROTS, PEELED AND CUT INTO ¼-INCH SLICES

2 STALKS CELERY, CUT INTO ¼-INCH SLICES

1½ CUPS TURKEY OR CHICKEN BROTH (TO MAKE HOMEMADE, SEE PAGE 17)

1 CUP FROZEN PEAS

2 CUPS (½-INCH PIECES) SKINLESS LEFTOVER COOKED TURKEY OR CHICKEN, CUT INTO ½-INCH PIECES (10 OUNCES)

⅓ CUP LOOSELY PACKED FRESH DILL, CHOPPED

1 Prepare shortcake biscuits: Preheat oven to 425°F. In medium bowl, combine baking powder, 1⅓ cups flour, ½ teaspoon salt, and ¼ teaspoon pepper. With pastry blender or 2 knives used scissor-fashion, cut in 3 tablespoons butter until mixture resembles coarse crumbs. Stir in ½ cup milk. By hand, knead mixture in bowl just until dough holds together.

2 On ungreased cookie sheet, with lightly floured hands, pat dough into 6-inch square. With sharp knife, cut dough into 4 squares. Arrange squares 2 inches apart on sheet. Bake biscuits 13 to 15 minutes.

3 Meanwhile, in saucepan, melt remaining 1 tablespoon butter over medium heat. Add onion and cook 5 minutes or until tender, stirring occasionally. Add carrots, celery, broth, remaining ½ teaspoon salt, and remaining ¼ teaspoon pepper; heat to boiling over high heat. Reduce heat to low and simmer 10 to 12 minutes or until vegetables are tender.

4 Whisk remaining 2 tablespoons flour into remaining ½ cup milk. In thin, steady stream, pour milk mixture into hot broth mixture, whisking constantly. Heat to boiling; boil 1 minute. Stir in frozen peas and turkey; heat through. Remove from heat; stir in dill. Serve shortcake-style: Split biscuits horizontally and spoon turkey mixture between halves.

EACH SERVING: ABOUT 490 CALORIES | 31G PROTEIN | 51G CARBOHYDRATE | 17G TOTAL FAT (4G SATURATED) | 5G FIBER | 61MG CHOLESTEROL | 1,065MG SODIUM

SALSA VERDE ENCHILADAS

Store-bought rotisserie chickens and salsa verde make these enchiladas a delicious weeknight fix; making an extra casserole to freeze for later saves even more time. With reduced-fat sour cream and cheese, we've lightened the calories, too.

ACTIVE TIME: 50 MINUTES · TOTAL TIME: 1 HOUR 10 MINUTES
MAKES: 2 CASSEROLES (4 MAIN-DISH SERVINGS EACH)

2	ROTISSERIE CHICKENS	16	(6-INCH) CORN TORTILLAS
2	JARS (16 TO 17.6 OUNCES EACH) MILD SALSA VERDE	1	CONTAINER (8 OUNCES) REDUCED-FAT SOUR CREAM
6	GREEN ONIONS, THINLY SLICED	¼	CUP REDUCED-SODIUM CHICKEN BROTH
¼	CUP FRESH LIME JUICE (FROM 2 TO 3 LIMES)	1	PACKAGE (8 OUNCES) REDUCED-FAT (2%) SHREDDED MEXICAN CHEESE BLEND (2 CUPS)
½	CUP LOOSELY PACKED FRESH CILANTRO LEAVES, CHOPPED		

1 Remove meat from chickens and coarsely shred; place in medium bowl (you will need 5½ cups); reserve any extra for another use). Discard skin and bones. Stir ½ cup salsa verde into chicken to evenly coat.

2 Preheat oven to 350°F. Grease two 13" by 9" glass or ceramic baking dishes; set aside. In 12-inch skillet, heat remaining salsa verde, green onions, and lime juice to boiling over medium-high heat. Boil 2 minutes, stirring occasionally. Stir in 2 tablespoons cilantro; keep warm over very low heat.

3 With tongs, place 1 tortilla in salsa verde mixture; heat 10 seconds. Place tortilla on waxed paper; top with about ⅓ cup shredded-chicken mixture. Roll up tortilla and place, seam side down, in prepared baking dish. Repeat with remaining tortillas and chicken mixture, arranging 8 tortillas in each dish.

4 Stir sour cream and broth into remaining salsa verde mixture in skillet; spoon over filled tortillas. Cover one baking dish with foil and bake 15 minutes. Remove foil; sprinkle with 1 cup cheese and 1 tablespoon cilantro. Bake 5 minutes longer or until cheese melts. Meanwhile, sprinkle remaining cheese and cilantro over second casserole and prepare for freezing.

EACH SERVING: ABOUT 465 CALORIES | 39G PROTEIN | 36G CARBOHYDRATE | 18G TOTAL FAT (7G SATURATED) | 3G FIBER | 117MG CHOLESTEROL | 785MG SODIUM

WINTER VEGETABLE POT PIE

Pairing hearty, homey vegetables with a white-wine-and-thyme sauce gives this cold-weather classic a subtle sophistication. Topping it all off: a no-fuss crust of golden-brown buttermilk biscuits.

ACTIVE TIME: 50 MINUTES · TOTAL TIME: 1 HOUR 40 MINUTES
MAKES: 4 MAIN-DISH SERVINGS

VEGETABLE FILLIING

4   MEDIUM CARROTS

1   LARGE RUSSET POTATO

1   LARGE SWEET POTATO

1   LARGE CELERY ROOT (1½ POUNDS)

1   JUMBO ONION (1 POUND), CUT INTO ¾-INCH CHUNKS

2   TABLESPOONS OLIVE OIL

1   TEASPOON FRESH THYME LEAVES, FINELY CHOPPED

¼   TEASPOON SALT

¼   TEASPOON FRESHLY GROUND BLACK PEPPER

1¾ CUPS REDUCED SODIUM CHICKEN BROTH (TO MAKE HOMEMADE, WHICH IS NATURALLY LOW SODIUM, SEE PAGE 17)

⅓   CUP DRY WHITE WINE

2   TABLESPOONS WATER

1   TABLESPOON CORNSTARCH

1   CUP FROZEN PEAS

¼   CUP HEAVY OR WHIPPING CREAM

BISCUIT TOPPING

1   CUP ALL-PURPOSE FLOUR

1½ TABLESPOONS BAKING POWDER

¼   TEASPOON BAKING SODA

1   TEASPOON FRESH THYME LEAVES, FINELY CHOPPED

¼   TEASPOON SALT

¼   TEASPOON FRESHLY GROUND BLACK PEPPER

2   TABLESPOONS BUTTER OR TRANS-FAT-FREE VEGETABLE SHORTENING

½   CUP LOW-FAT BUTTERMILK

1   TABLESPOON FRESH DILL, CHOPPED

1   Prepare Vegetable Filling: Preheat oven to 425°F. Peel and cut carrots, potatoes, and celery root into ¾-inch pieces. In 15½" by 10½" jelly-roll pan, combine onion, carrots, potatoes, celery root, oil, thyme, salt, and pepper. Toss to coat; spread in even layer. Roast 50 minutes to 1 hour or until vegetables are browned and tender, stirring once halfway through roasting.

2   Meanwhile, in 4-quart saucepan, heat broth and wine to boiling over medium-high heat. In small bowl, mix water and cornstarch until blended. Reduce heat to medium and stir in cornstarch mixture. Cook 3 to 4 minutes or until liquid thickens, stirring frequently. Stir in peas and roasted vegetables, then cook 2 to 3 minutes to heat through. Remove from heat and stir in cream.

3   Spoon vegetable mixture into 8" by 8" ceramic or glass baking dish, spreading mixture evenly.

4   Prepare Biscuit Topping: In large bowl, combine flour, baking powder, baking soda, thyme, salt, and pepper until well blended. With pastry blender or 2 knives used scissors-fashion, cut in butter until coarse crumbs form. With fork, stir in buttermilk just until mixture forms a dough. With tablespoon, scoop generous spoonful into floured palm. With floured hands, gently pat into 2-inch round (½ inch thick) and place on top of vegetable mixture. Repeat with remaining dough, spacing rounds ½ inch apart. (There should be 12 biscuits on top.)

5   Bake 16 to 20 minutes or until biscuits are puffed and golden brown and filling is bubbling. Cool in pan on wire rack 10 minutes. Sprinkle with chopped dill and serve.

EACH SERVING: ABOUT 495 CALORIES | 11G PROTEIN | 71G CARBOHYDRATE | 20G TOTAL FAT (9G SATURATED) | 9G FIBER | 38MG CHOLESTEROL | 920MG SODIUM

CURRIED SWEET POTATO SHEPHERD'S PIE

Our adaptation of shepherd's pie delivers a formidable combination of curry-spiked turkey, gingered vegetables, and mashed sweet potatoes.

ACTIVE TIME: 1 HOUR · TOTAL TIME: 2 HOURS 20 MINUTES

MAKES: 2 CASSEROLES, 6 MAIN-DISH SERVINGS EACH

---

5 MEDIUM SWEET POTATOES (12 OUNCES EACH; SEE TIP)	1½ POUNDS PARSNIPS, PEELED AND CHOPPED
2 TABLESPOONS VEGETABLE OIL	1 MEDIUM ONION, CHOPPED
2 POUNDS GROUND TURKEY OR CHICKEN	1 TABLESPOON GRATED, PEELED FRESH GINGER
2 TEASPOONS SALT	1 BAG (10 OUNCES) FROZEN PEAS
⅓ CUP ALL-PURPOSE FLOUR	1 CUP REDUCED-FAT MILK (2%), WARMED
1 TABLESPOON CURRY POWDER	
1¾ CUPS CHICKEN BROTH (TO MAKE HOMEMADE, SEE PAGE 17)	2 TABLESPOONS BUTTER OR MARGARINE
1½ POUNDS CARROTS, PEELED AND CHOPPED	

1 Pierce sweet potatoes all over with fork. Microwave on High 15 to 17 minutes, until tender when pierced, turning over once.

2 In 12-inch skillet, heat 1 tablespoon oil over medium-high heat until hot. Add turkey. Sprinkle with ½ teaspoon salt and cook 5 minutes or until no longer pink, stirring and breaking up turkey with side of spoon.

3 Stir flour and curry powder into turkey in skillet; cook 1 minute, stirring. Add broth; heat to boiling. Cook 1 minute or until mixture thickens slightly. Divide turkey mixture between two 2½- to 3-quart baking dishes and spread evenly.

4 Preheat oven to 375°F. Wipe skillet dry; add remaining 1 tablespoon oil and heat over medium heat until hot. Add carrots, parsnips, and onion; cook, covered, stirring occasionally, until vegetables are browned and tender, about 15 minutes. Stir in ginger, frozen peas, and ½ teaspoon salt. Divide vegetables between casseroles, spreading over turkey.

5 Scoop sweet-potato flesh into bowl and coarsely mash. Stir in milk, butter, and remaining 1 teaspoon salt; mash until well blended. Spread sweet-potato mixture over vegetables.

6 Bake, uncovered, 35 to 40 minutes or until top is browned.

TIP When microwaving sweet potatoes, pick ones that are as uniform in size and shape as possible—otherwise they won't cook evenly.

EACH SERVING: ABOUT 365 CALORIES | 19G PROTEIN | 47G CARBOHYDRATE | 12G TOTAL FAT (3G SATURATED) | 9G FIBER | 61MG CHOLESTEROL | 630MG SODIUM

POLENTA CASSEROLE

This Italian casserole delivers comfort with creamy polenta and a hearty tomato ragu studded with spicy sausage and eggplant.

ACTIVE TIME: 40 MINUTES · **TOTAL TIME:** 2 HOURS
MAKES: 2 CASSEROLES, 4 MAIN-DISH SERVINGS EACH

12 OUNCES HOT ITALIAN TURKEY SAUSAGE, CASINGS REMOVED	4 CUPS WATER
12 OUNCES MEAT-LOAF MIX (VEAL, PORK, AND BEEF) OR GROUND BEEF CHUCK	1¾ CUPS CHICKEN BROTH (TO MAKE HOMEMADE, SEE PAGE 17)
1 JUMBO ONION (1 POUND), CHOPPED	1½ CUPS CORNMEAL
2 GARLIC CLOVES, FINELY CHOPPED	½ TEASPOON SALT
1 CAN (28 OUNCES) WHOLE TOMATOES IN PUREE	¾ CUP FRESHLY GRATED PECORINO-ROMANO OR PARMESAN CHEESE
1 SMALL EGGPLANT (1 POUND), CUT INTO ½-INCH PIECES	

1 In 5- to 6-quart Dutch oven, cook sausage and meat-loaf mix over medium-high heat 5 to 6 minutes or until browned, breaking up meat with side of spoon. With slotted spoon, transfer meat mixture to medium bowl.

2 To same Dutch oven, add onion; cook over medium heat 8 to 10 minutes or until tender. Stir in garlic; cook 30 seconds. Add tomatoes with their puree; heat to boiling over high heat, breaking up tomatoes with side of spoon. Reduce heat and simmer, uncovered, 10 minutes. Add eggplant and meat; cover and cook 5 minutes over medium heat. Uncover and cook, stirring occasionally, until eggplant is tender, about 10 minutes longer.

3 Prepare polenta: In microwave-safe 4-quart bowl, with wire whisk, combine water, broth, cornmeal, and salt. Microwave on High 15 to 20 minutes or until cornmeal mixture is very thick. After first 5 minutes of cooking, whisk vigorously until smooth; then whisk 2 more times during remaining cooking time. Remove from microwave; whisk in Pecorino.

4 Meanwhile, preheat oven to 400°F. Spoon 2 cups hot polenta into each of two 1½-quart shallow casseroles. Spread polenta over bottom and up sides of casseroles. Spoon eggplant and meat filling over polenta. Spread remaining polenta around casserole edge to form a rim.

5 Bake 30 minutes or until hot. Let stand 10 minutes for easier serving.

EACH SERVING: ABOUT 385 CALORIES | 22G PROTEIN | 34G CARBOHYDRATE | 18G TOTAL FAT (7G SATURATED) | 6G FIBER | 65MG CHOLESTEROL | 1,045 MG SODIUM

CHILI POT PIE WITH POLENTA CRUST

Polenta is the ultimate quick-dinner trick. Cornmeal simmered in the microwave in a mixture of water and milk becomes a creamy crust for a fun and tasty chili pot pie.

ACTIVE TIME: 30 MINUTES · TOTAL TIME: 2 HOURS 20 MINUTES PLUS STANDING
MAKES: 10 MAIN-DISH SERVINGS

CHILI

2 TEASPOONS OLIVE OIL

1½ POUNDS WELL-TRIMMED BONELESS BEEF CHUCK, CUT INTO ½-INCH PIECES

¾ TEASPOON SALT

1 MEDIUM ONION, CHOPPED

1 MEDIUM RED PEPPER, CHOPPED

3 GARLIC CLOVES, CRUSHED WITH GARLIC PRESS

1 SERRANO OR JALAPEÑO CHILE, SEEDED AND FINELY CHOPPED

2 TABLESPOONS TOMATO PASTE

3 TABLESPOONS CHILI POWDER

1 TABLESPOON GROUND CUMIN

1 CAN (28 OUNCES) WHOLE TOMATOES IN JUICE

2 CANS (15 TO 19 OUNCES EACH) RED KIDNEY BEANS, RINSED AND DRAINED

POLENTA CRUST

2 CUPS LOW-FAT MILK (1%)

1½ CUPS CORNMEAL

¾ TEASPOON SALT

4½ CUPS BOILING WATER

1 Prepare chili: In 12-inch skillet with broiler-safe handle, heat oil over medium-high heat until hot. Sprinkle beef with ¼ teaspoon salt.

2 Add beef to skillet in 2 batches and cook 4 to 5 minutes per batch or until beef is browned on all sides, stirring occasionally and adding more oil if necessary. With slotted spoon, transfer beef to bowl when it is browned.

3 After all beef is browned, add onion, red pepper, garlic, and serrano to same skillet and cook over medium heat, stirring occasionally, until all vegetables are lightly browned and tender, about 8 minutes. Stir in tomato paste, chili powder, cumin, and remaining ½ teaspoon salt; cook 1 minute, stirring constantly.

4 Return beef and any juices in bowl to skillet. Add tomatoes with their juice, stirring and breaking up tomatoes with side of spoon; heat to boiling over medium-high heat.

5   Reduce heat to low; cover and simmer 1 hour and 15 minutes, stirring occasionally. Add beans and cook, uncovered, 15 minutes longer or until meat is tender.

6   Meanwhile, prepare polenta crust: After adding beans to chili, in microwave-safe deep 4-quart bowl or casserole, combine milk, cornmeal, and salt until blended; whisk in boiling water.

7   Cook in microwave on High 12 to 15 minutes. After first 5 minutes of cooking, whisk vigorously until smooth (mixture will be lumpy at first). Stir 2 more times during cooking. While polenta is cooking, preheat broiler.

8   When chili is done, skim off and discard fat. Spread polenta evenly over chili in skillet. Place skillet in broiler 6 to 8 inches from source of heat and broil 3 to 4 minutes or until polenta crust is lightly browned, rotating skillet if necessary for even browning. Let pie stand 10 minutes for easier serving.

EACH SERVING: ABOUT 335 CALORIES | 26G PROTEIN | 44G CARBOHYDRATE | 7G TOTAL FAT (2G SATURATED) | 11G FIBER | 34MG CHOLESTEROL | 780MG SODIUM

SPICY SAUSAGE JAMBALAYA

This hearty Creole classic is slimmed down with chicken tenders and turkey sausage (in place of high-fat pork). Brown rice boosts the fiber and key phytonutrients, while peppers and tomatoes deliver half the daily recommendation of vitamin C—and it's all cooked in one skillet!

ACTIVE TIME: 10 MINUTES · TOTAL TIME: 25 MINUTES
MAKES: 4 MAIN-DISH SERVINGS

8   OUNCES TURKEY ANDOUILLE SAUSAGE, CUT INTO ¼-INCH SLICES

1   GREEN OR YELLOW PEPPER, CHOPPED

1   CAN (14½ OUNCES) STEWED TOMATOES

1   CUP UNCOOKED INSTANT BROWN RICE

8   OUNCES CHICKEN TENDERS, EACH CUT CROSSWISE IN HALF

½   CUP WATER

¼   TEASPOON SALT

1   BUNCH GREEN ONIONS, SLICED

1   Heat 12-inch skillet over medium heat until hot. Add sausage and green pepper and cook 5 minutes, stirring occasionally.

2   Stir in tomatoes with their juice, rice, chicken, water, and salt; heat to boiling over high heat. Reduce heat to low; cover and simmer 10 minutes or until rice is tender.

3   Remove skillet from heat; stir in green onions.

EACH SERVING: ABOUT 265 CALORIES | 26G PROTEIN | 30G CARBOHYDRATE | 6G TOTAL FAT (2G SATURATED) | 4G FIBER | 73MG CHOLESTEROL | 830MG SODIUM

CAJUN MEAT LOAF

For a soul-satisfying meal, pair up with Mashed Potatoes with Browned Onions (page 107) and New Green Bean Casserole (page 116).

ACTIVE TIME: 20 MINUTES · TOTAL TIME: 1 HOUR 35 MINUTES
MAKES: 8 MAIN-DISH SERVINGS

---

2   TABLESPOONS BUTTER OR MARGARINE

2   CARROTS, PEELED AND FINELY CHOPPED

1   LARGE ONION (12 OUNCES), CHOPPED

1   LARGE STALK CELERY, CHOPPED

1   SMALL GREEN PEPPER, FINELY CHOPPED

2   GARLIC CLOVES, CRUSHED WITH GARLIC PRESS

2   POUNDS GROUND MEAT FOR MEAT LOAF (BEEF, PORK, AND VEAL)

2   LARGE EGGS

1   CUP FRESH BREAD CRUMBS (ABOUT 2 SLICES BREAD)

½   CUP PLUS 2 TABLESPOONS KETCHUP

¼   CUP MILK

1   TABLESPOON WORCESTERSHIRE SAUCE

2   TEASPOONS SALT

1   TEASPOON GROUND CUMIN

½   TEASPOON DRIED THYME

½   TEASPOON GROUND NUTMEG

½   TEASPOON CAYENNE (GROUND RED PEPPER)

½   TEASPOON COARSELY GROUND BLACK PEPPER

1 In nonstick 12-inch skillet, melt butter over medium heat. Add carrots, onion, celery, and green pepper and cook, stirring occasionally, until vegetables are tender, about 15 minutes. Add garlic and cook 1 minute longer. Set aside to cool slightly.

2 Preheat oven to 375°F. In large bowl, combine ground meat, eggs, bread crumbs, ½ cup ketchup, milk, Worcestershire, salt, cumin, thyme, nutmeg, ground red pepper, black pepper, and cooked vegetable mixture just until well blended but not overmixed.

3 In 13" by 9" baking pan, shape meat mixture into 10" by 5" loaf, pressing firmly. Brush remaining 2 tablespoons ketchup on top of loaf. Bake 1 hour 15 minutes. Let stand 10 minutes to set juices for easier slicing.

EACH SERVING: ABOUT 365 CALORIES | 24G PROTEIN | 14G CARBOHYDRATE | 23G TOTAL FAT (10G SATURATED) | 149MG CHOLESTEROL | 961MG SODIUM

SANDWICHES & PIZZAS

For lunch, a casual supper, or a hearty snack, sink your teeth into these between-the bread favorites. A plump, juicy burger with all the fixings or a rotisserie-chicken barbecue sandwich are sure to satisfy. BLTS are made new again with the addition of grilled salmon, while an old-fashioned tuna melt is updated with a side of carrot-raisin slaw.

If you're hankering for something warm and cheesy, we have lots of options: three kinds of panini, each featuring a favorite melting cheese, plus a tortilla pie and chicken quesadillas that use a reduced-fat Mexican cheese blend and low-fat tortillas, if you choose. For pizza lovers, we have two amazingly easy to make options—a spicy sausage calzone and a hero sandwich-style pizza. Both take advantage of time-savers like refrigerated pizza dough and bottled marinara sauce for comfort food in a jiffy.

The Perfect Burger (recipe on page 88)

THE PERFECT BURGER

What could be more irresistible than a big, juicy burger with all the fixings? For photo, see page 86.

ACTIVE TIME: 10 MINUTES · TOTAL TIME: 18 MINUTES
MAKES: 4 BURGERS

---

4   (12-INCH) BAMBOO SKEWERS

1¼ POUNDS GROUND BEEF CHUCK

½   TEASPOON COARSELY GROUND BLACK PEPPER

1   TEASPOON SALT

1   LARGE SWEET ONION (12 OUNCES), SUCH AS VIDALIA OR MAUI, CUT INTO ½-INCH-THICK ROUNDS

4   HAMBURGER BUNS, SPLIT

4   GREEN-LEAF LETTUCE LEAVES

2   RIPE MEDIUM TOMATOES (6 TO 8 OUNCES EACH), THINLY SLICED

1   Soak skewers in water to cover 15 minutes. Meanwhile, prepare outdoor grill for covered direct grilling over medium heat, or preheat ridged grill pan over medium heat until very hot.

2   Shape ground beef into 4 equal patties (see Tip). Sprinkle pepper and ¾ teaspoon salt on both sides of patties. Thread 1 skewer through center of each onion slice. Sprinkle onion with remaining ¼ teaspoon salt.

3   Place burgers and onion on hot grill; cook 8 to 10 minutes for medium or to desired doneness, turning over once. Onion should be browned and tender. About 1 minute before the burgers are done, add buns, cut sides down, to grill. Grill just until toasted.

4   Serve burgers on buns with lettuce, tomato, and onion.

TIP For best results, handle the ground beef as little as possible, shaping your burgers without compacting them too much.

EACH BURGER: ABOUT 485 CALORIES | 31G PROTEIN | 33G CARBOHYDRATE | 25G TOTAL FAT (9G SATURATED) | 96MG CHOLESTEROL | 920MG SODIUM

TUNA MELTS WITH CARROT-RAISIN SALAD

These quick and easy tuna melts will make you feel nostalgic. For a more traditional carrot salad, replace the cumin with cinnamon. You can also substitute dried cranberries or other dried fruits for the raisins.

ACTIVE TIME: 5 MINUTES · TOTAL TIME: 10 MINUTES
MAKES: 4 SANDWICHES

TUNA MELT

- 1 CAN (12 OUNCES) SOLID WHITE TUNA IN WATER, DRAINED
- 1 STALK CELERY, THINLY SLICED
- ¼ CUP REDUCED-FAT MAYONNAISE
- 1 TABLESPOON BUTTER OR MARGARINE
- 8 SLICES RYE BREAD (ABOUT 8 OUNCES TOTAL)
- 4 OUNCES SLICED CHEDDAR CHEESE OR SWISS CHEESE

CARROT-RAISIN SALAD

- 1 CONTAINER (8 OUNCES) PLAIN LOW-FAT YOGURT
- 1 BAG (10 OUNCES) SHREDDED CARROTS
- ½ CUP RAISINS
- ⅛ TEASPOON GROUND CUMIN
- ⅛ TEASPOON SALT

1   Prepare Tuna Melt: In small bowl, with fork, combine tuna, celery, and mayonnaise.

2   In nonstick 12-inch skillet, melt butter over medium heat. Meanwhile, spread tuna mixture evenly on 4 bread slices. Top each with one-fourth of Cheddar and a remaining slice of bread.

3   Arrange sandwiches in skillet. Cover skillet; cook 5 minutes or until Cheddar melts and bread is toasted, turning sandwiches over once.

4   While sandwiches are cooking, prepare Carrot-Raisin Salad: In small bowl, stir yogurt, carrots, raisins, cumin, and salt until combined. Makes about 4 cups.

5   Serve each tuna melt with a scoop of Carrot-Raisin Salad.

EACH SANDWICH: ABOUT 440 CALORIES | 31G PROTEIN | 33G CARBOHYDRATE | 20G TOTAL FAT (7G SATURATED) | 4G FIBER | 61MG CHOLESTEROL | 1,055MG SODIUM

SALMON BLTS WITH LEMON-DILL MAYONNAISE

Here's a toothsome take on everyone's favorite sandwich. Keep the skin on salmon fillets when grilling to prevent them from falling apart.

ACTIVE TIME: 15 MINUTES · **TOTAL TIME:** 26 MINUTES

MAKES: 4 SANDWICHES

⅓ CUP LIGHT MAYONNAISE

2 TEASPOONS CHOPPED FRESH DILL

1 TEASPOON FRESHLY GRATED LEMON PEEL

4 PIECES SALMON FILLET WITH SKIN ON, 1 INCH THICK (ABOUT 6 OUNCES EACH)

¼ TEASPOON SALT

⅛ TEASPOON COARSELY GROUND BLACK PEPPER

8 CENTER SLICES (½ INCH THICK) COUNTRY-STYLE BREAD

4 ROMAINE LETTUCE LEAVES

2 RIPE MEDIUM TOMATOES (6 TO 8 OUNCES EACH), SLICED

6 SLICES BACON, COOKED UNTIL CRISP AND EACH BROKEN IN HALF

1   Lightly grease grill rack. Prepare outdoor grill for covered direct grilling over medium heat.

2   In small bowl, stir mayonnaise, dill, and lemon peel until mixed; set aside. Sprinkle salmon with salt and pepper.

3   Place salmon, skin side down, on hot grill rack over medium heat. Cover grill and cook until salmon is opaque throughout, 10 to 12 minutes, without turning over. Slide thin metal spatula between salmon flesh and skin. Lift salmon from skin and transfer to plate; discard skin if you like. Meanwhile, place bread on grill rack with salmon and cook about 1 minute on each side, until lightly toasted.

4   Spread lemon-dill mayonnaise on 1 side of toasted bread slices. Place 1 lettuce leaf, folding to fit, on each of 4 bread slices. Top each with 2 or 3 tomato slices, 1 salmon fillet, 3 pieces of bacon, and another bread slice.

EACH SERVING: ABOUT 570 CALORIES | 44G PROTEIN | 41G CARBOHYDRATE | 24G TOTAL FAT (5G SATURATED) | 3G FIBER | 108MG CHOLESTEROL | 955MG SODIUM

CARAMELIZED ONION AND GOAT CHEESE PANINI

With savory seasonal fillings and a flame-charred crunch, these melty sandwiches are grilled cheese for grown-ups. A heavy skillet does the work of a panini maker to hot-press the ingredients together.

ACTIVE TIME: 5 MINUTES · TOTAL TIME: 50 MINUTES
MAKES: 8 APPETIZER SERVINGS

2 TABLESPOONS OLIVE OIL

2 SWEET ONIONS (1 POUND EACH), THINLY SLICED

½ TEASPOON SALT

¼ TEASPOON GROUND BLACK PEPPER

½ TEASPOON CHOPPED FRESH THYME LEAVES

8 CENTER SLICES (½ INCH THICK) COUNTRY-STYLE BREAD

4 OUNCES SOFT FRESH GOAT CHEESE

1 In nonstick 12-inch skillet, heat oil over medium heat 1 minute. Stir in onions, salt, and pepper; cover and cook 15 minutes or until very soft, stirring occasionally. Uncover and cook, stirring frequently, until onions are golden brown, 15 to 25 minutes longer. Stir in thyme; remove skillet from heat.

2 Prepare outdoor grill or grill pan for direct grilling over medium heat.

3 Meanwhile, assemble panini: Place 4 slices of bread on work surface. Spread one fourth of goat cheese on each bread slice and top each with one fourth of onion mixture. Top with remaining bread slices.

4 Place 2 panini on hot grill grate. Place heavy skillet (preferably cast iron) on top of panini, press down, and cook 7 to 8 minutes or until bread is toasted and browned on both sides, turning over once. Repeat with remaining 2 panini. Cut panini into halves or quarters to serve.

EACH SERVING: ABOUT 190 CALORIES | 7G PROTEIN | 24G CARBOHYDRATE | 8G TOTAL FAT (3G SATURATED) | 3G FIBER | 7MG CHOLESTEROL | 375MG SODIUM

RED PEPPER AND PROVOLONE PANINI

Prepare panini as above, but omit step 1. In step 2, while grill is preheating, in small bowl, combine **1 jar (7 ounces) roasted red peppers**, drained and sliced; **¼ cup white wine vinegar**; **1 clove garlic**, crushed with press; and **¼ teaspoon freshly ground black pepper**. Set aside 10 minutes; drain. In step 3, divide **6 ounces sliced provolone, 4 ounces sliced Genoa salami**, and marinated red peppers evenly among **4 bread slices**; top with remaining bread. Complete as described in step 4.

EACH SERVING: ABOUT 215 CALORIES | 11G PROTEIN | 17G CARBOHYDRATE | 11G TOTAL FAT (5G SATURATED FAT) | 1G FIBER | 28MG CHOLESTEROL | 675MG SODIUM

MOZZARELLA, TOMATO, AND BASIL PANINI

Prepare panini as above but omit step 1. In step 3, divide **2 ripe plum tomatoes**, cored and sliced; **6 ounces fresh mozzarella**, sliced; **½ cup loosely packed fresh basil leaves**; **⅛ teaspoon salt**; and **¼ teaspoon freshly ground black pepper** evenly among **4 bread slices**. Top with remaining bread. Complete as described in step 4.

EACH SERVING: ABOUT 145 CALORIES | 7G PROTEIN | 17G CARBOHYDRATE | 6G TOTAL FAT (3G SATURATED FAT) | 1G FIBER | 17MG CHOLESTEROL | 230MG SODIUM

PULLED-CHICKEN SANDWICHES

Transform rotisserie chicken into a tangy, barbecue-sauced sandwich filling with this quick and easy recipe.

ACTIVE TIME: 10 MINUTES · TOTAL TIME: 15 MINUTES
MAKES: 6 MAIN-DISH SERVINGS

1   SMALL ROTISSERIE CHICKEN
    (2 TO 2½ POUNDS)
1   CUP BARBECUE SAUCE
½   CUP WATER
¼   CUP RED WINE VINEGAR

6   KAISER ROLLS, SPLIT
8   OUNCES DELI COLESLAW
CARROT AND CELERY STICKS

1   Remove skin and bones from chicken; coarsely shred meat.
2   In 2-quart saucepan, combine chicken, barbecue sauce, water, and vinegar. Cook over medium heat 5 minutes or until hot, stirring frequently.
3   Spoon chicken mixture onto bottom half of each roll, then top each with coleslaw and other half of roll.
4   Serve with assorted carrot and celery sticks.

EACH SERVING: ABOUT 405 CALORIES | 34G PROTEIN | 40G CARBOHYDRATE | 11G TOTAL FAT (3G SATURATED) | 2G FIBER | 87MG CHOLESTEROL | 870MG SODIUM

CHICKEN QUESADILLAS WITH AVOCADO SALSA

This tasty Tex-Mex uses lower-fat tortillas and cheese. The splurge: avocado. Though high in fat, it's mostly the heart-healthy kind; plus, avocados contain a natural cholesterol reducer.

ACTIVE TIME: 10 MINUTES · TOTAL TIME: 35 MINUTES
MAKES: 4 MAIN-DISH SERVINGS

2   TEASPOONS CANOLA OIL

1   GREEN ONION, THINLY SLICED

1   LIME

1   POUND SKINLESS, BONELESS THIN-SLICED CHICKEN BREASTS, CUT INTO 1-INCH STRIPS

¼   TEASPOON SALT

⅛   TEASPOON GROUND BLACK PEPPER

4   BURRITO-SIZE LOW-FAT FLOUR TORTILLAS

1   CUP REDUCED-FAT SHREDDED MEXICAN CHEESE BLEND

½   AVOCADO, PEELED, SEEDED, AND CUT INTO ½-INCH PIECES

¾   CUP SALSA

1   In nonstick 12-inch skillet, heat oil over medium heat 1 minute. Add green onion and cook, stirring occasionally, until tender, about 6 minutes.

2   Meanwhile, from lime, grate 1 teaspoon peel and squeeze 2 tablespoons juice. Season chicken strips on both sides with lime peel, salt, and pepper.

3   Add chicken to green onion in skillet; cook 10 minutes or until chicken is no longer pink inside. Transfer chicken and green onion to bowl; stir in lime juice.

4   Evenly divide chicken mixture and cheese among tortillas, placing it on one half of each; fold over to make 4 quesadillas.

5   In same skillet, cook quesadillas over medium heat, in 2 batches, 7 to 8 minutes per batch or until browned on both sides and heated through. Cut each quesadilla into thirds. Stir avocado into salsa; serve with quesadillas.

EACH SERVING: ABOUT 400 CALORIES | 38G PROTEIN | 31G CARBOHYDRATE | 14G TOTAL FAT (5G SATURATED) | 8G FIBER | 86MG CHOLESTEROL | 970MG SODIUM

CORN AND BLACK BEAN TORTILLA PIE

We've slimmed down this comfort food classic by using reduced-fat shredded cheese and by packing the filling with low-calorie ingredients like corn and black beans.

ACTIVE TIME: 5 MINUTES · **TOTAL TIME:** 20 MINUTES
MAKES: 4 MAIN-DISH SERVINGS

1   CUP FROZEN CORN KERNELS

2   GREEN ONIONS, THINLY SLICED

1   TEASPOON GROUND CUMIN

1½ CUPS SALSA

1   CAN (15 TO 19 OUNCES) LOW-SODIUM BLACK BEANS, RINSED AND DRAINED

4   BURRITO-SIZE FLOUR TORTILLAS

1   PACKAGE (8 OUNCES) REDUCED-FAT SHREDDED MEXICAN CHEESE BLEND

2   TABLESPOONS FRESH CILANTRO LEAVES, CHOPPED

1   Preheat oven to 450°F. Spray large cookie sheet with nonstick cooking spray.

2   Spray 12-inch skillet with cooking spray; place over medium heat. Add corn, green onions, and cumin; cook 3 minutes or until corn thaws. Remove skillet from heat; stir in salsa and beans.

3   Place 1 tortilla on cookie sheet; top with 1 cup bean mixture and ½ cup cheese. Repeat, starting with tortilla, to make 2 more layers. Top with remaining tortilla and cheese.

4   Bake pie 9 to 10 minutes or until heated through. Carefully transfer pie to a cutting board, then sprinkle with cilantro. With sharp knife, cut pie into wedges and serve.

EACH SERVING: ABOUT 440 CALORIES | 26G PROTEIN | 58G CARBOHYDRATE | 13G TOTAL FAT (6G SATURATED) | 21G FIBER | 41MG CHOLESTEROL | 1,105MG SODIUM

SAUSAGE CALZONES

Hot from the oven, this express-lane meal utilizes refrigerated pizza dough, bottled marinara sauce, and zesty chicken sausage.

ACTIVE TIME: 10 MINUTES · TOTAL TIME: 35 MINUTES
MAKES: 4 MAIN-DISH SERVINGS

1   CUP PART-SKIM RICOTTA CHEESE

1   LINK (3 OUNCES) FULLY COOKED ITALIAN CHICKEN SAUSAGE, CUT INTO CUBES

¾   CUP FROZEN PEAS

½   CUP SHREDDED PART-SKIM MOZZARELLA CHEESE

1   TUBE (13.8 OUNCES) REFRIGERATED PIZZA DOUGH

1   CUP MARINARA SAUCE, WARMED

1   Preheat oven to 400°F. In medium bowl, stir together ricotta, sausage, frozen peas, and mozzarella.

2   Spray large cookie sheet with nonstick cooking spray. Unroll pizza dough on center of cookie sheet. With fingertips, press dough into 14" by 10" rectangle. Cut dough lengthwise in half, then cut each piece crosswise in half to make 4 rectangles.

3   Place one fourth ricotta filling on half of one dough rectangle. Fold other half of dough over filling and pinch edges together to seal. Repeat with remaining filling and dough.

4   Bake 25 minutes or until well browned on top. Serve with marinara sauce for dipping.

EACH SERVING: ABOUT 485 CALORIES | 25G PROTEIN | 59G CARBOHYDRATE | 16G TOTAL FAT (7G SATURATED) | 4G FIBER | 51MG CHOLESTEROL | 1,210MG SODIUM

HERO PIZZA

We've gathered all of the best ingredients from a hot and saucy hero sandwich—Italian sausage, peppers, and plenty of cheese—and put them on a kid-friendly pizza.

ACTIVE TIME: 15 MINUTES · TOTAL TIME: 50 MINUTES
MAKES: 4 MAIN-DISH SERVINGS

1   TABLESPOON PLUS 1 TEASPOON OLIVE OIL

8   OUNCES ITALIAN TURKEY SAUSAGE, CASINGS REMOVED

1   MEDIUM RED PEPPER, THINLY SLICED

1   MEDIUM YELLOW PEPPER, THINLY SLICED

8   OUNCES (1 PACKAGE) SLICED MUSHROOMS

¼   TEASPOON SALT

⅛   TEASPOON GROUND BLACK PEPPER

1   POUND FRESH OR FROZEN (THAWED) PIZZA DOUGH

¾   CUP BOTTLED MARINARA SAUCE

1¼ CUPS SHREDDED PART-SKIM MOZZARELLA CHEESE (5 OUNCES)

¼   CUP FRESHLY GRATED PARMESAN CHEESE

1   Preheat oven to 450°F. Grease 15½" by 10½" jelly-roll pan with 1 table-spoon oil.

2   In nonstick 12-inch skillet, heat remaining 1 teaspoon oil over medium heat 1 minute. Add sausage; cook 6 to 8 minutes or until cooked through, breaking up sausage with side of spoon. With slotted spoon, transfer sausage to bowl.

3   To drippings in skillet, add red and yellow peppers and cook, covered, over medium heat 3 to 4 minutes or until tender, stirring occasionally. Add mushrooms and cook, uncovered, 6 to 8 minutes, stirring occasionally.

4   Return sausage to skillet; stir in salt and black pepper. Remove skillet from heat.

5   With fingers, push dough onto bottom and up sides of prepared pan. Spread marinara sauce over dough, then top with sausage mixture, mozzarella, and Parmesan. Place pan on rack in lower third of oven. Bake pizza 20 to 22 minutes or until topping is hot and bubbly and crust is browned.

EACH SERVING: ABOUT 615 CALORIES | 28G PROTEIN | 61G CARBOHYDRATE | 33G TOTAL FAT (10G SATURATED) | 4G FIBER | 54MG CHOLESTEROL | 1,285MG SODIUM

SATISFYING SIDES

A meat loaf is always better when served with mashed potatoes, and a burger is at its best with a side of fries. That's why we've shared our favorite potato recipes, from smooth and creamy smashed potatoes (and a sweet potato option, too) to potato pancakes and crispy fries that are baked rather than fried for lightness.

These side acts are so good everyone will be asking for seconds—or thirds. But the show doesn't stop with potatoes: Try our classic stuffing and a new lighter take on green bean casserole for the holidays or anytime you crave them. A piping hot gratin, creamed spinach, and sweet corn on the cob are also part of our comfort food buffet—main dish optional!

Oven Frites (recipe on page 112)

MASHED POTATOES WITH BROWNED ONIONS

A caramelized onion topping makes mashed potatoes even more irresistible. Who knew that was possible?

ACTIVE TIME: 15 MINUTES · **TOTAL TIME:** 50 MINUTES
MAKES: 6 SIDE-DISH SERVINGS

3   TABLESPOONS BUTTER

1   POUND SPANISH ONIONS (ABOUT 3 MEDIUM), EACH CUT IN HALF, THEN THINLY SLICED

2   TEASPOONS CIDER VINEGAR

3   MEDIUM BAKING POTATOES (ABOUT 8 OUNCES), PEELED, EACH CUT INTO QUARTERS

½   CUP WHOLE MILK, WARMED

¾   TEASPOON SALT

¼   TEASPOON GROUND BLACK PEPPER

1   In 12-inch skillet, melt butter over medium-low heat. Add onions, stirring to coat. Cover and cook 10 minutes or until onions soften, stirring occasionally. Uncover; increase heat to medium and cook 15 minutes longer or until onions are very soft, browned, and reduced to ¾ cup, stirring frequently. Stir in vinegar and set aside.

2   Meanwhile, in 3-quart saucepan, place potatoes and enough *water* to cover; heat to boiling over high heat. Reduce heat to low; cover and simmer 15 to 20 minutes or until potatoes are tender. Reserve ¼ *cup potato cooking water*. Drain potatoes.

3   In saucepan, with potato masher, mash potatoes until smooth. Gradually add warm milk, mashing potatoes until fluffy. Add some reserved potato cooking water if necessary. Stir in salt and pepper.

4   Spoon mashed potatoes into bowl; top with onion mixture. Stir before serving.

TIP   Consider making extra browned onions—they may be as popular as the potatoes!

EACH SERVING: ABOUT 175 CALORIES | 3G PROTEIN | 27G CARBOHYDRATE | 7G TOTAL FAT (2G SATURATED) | 3G FIBER | 3MG CHOLESTEROL | 385MG SODIUM

MASHED SWEET POTATOES

You don't have to wait until the holidays to enjoy this delectable side dish. A few tablespoons of soy sauce add a sweet, earthy flavor to our rendition of this favorite.

ACTIVE TIME: 10 MINUTES · **TOTAL TIME:** 20 MINUTES
MAKES: 12 SIDE-DISH SERVINGS

4   POUNDS SWEET POTATOES
    (5 MEDIUM), PEELED AND CUT INTO
    1½-INCH CHUNKS

4   TABLESPOONS BUTTER OR
    MARGARINE

3   TABLESPOONS SOY SAUCE

1   GREEN ONION, THINLY SLICED

1   In 5- or 6-quart saucepot, place sweet potatoes and enough *water* to cover; heat to boiling over high heat. Reduce heat to medium-low; cover and cook 10 to 12 minutes or until potatoes are tender. Drain well and set potatoes aside.

2   In same saucepot, melt butter over medium heat. Remove saucepot from heat; add soy sauce and potatoes. With potato masher, mash potatoes until almost smooth. Transfer to serving bowl and sprinkle with sliced green onions.

EACH SERVING: ABOUT 150 CALORIES | 2G PROTEIN | 27G CARBOHYDRATE | 4G TOTAL FAT (1G SATURATED) | 3G FIBER | 0MG CHOLESTEROL | 310MG SODIUM

POTATO GRATIN WITH GRUYÈRE

This classic French side dish (made with nutty Gruyère cheese) is well suited to accompany roasted meat or poultry.

ACTIVE TIME: 15 MINUTES · **TOTAL TIME:** 50 MINUTES
MAKES: 4 SIDE-DISH SERVINGS

1   CUP HALF-AND-HALF OR LIGHT CREAM

⅛ TEASPOON CAYENNE (GROUND RED) PEPPER

½ TEASPOON SALT

1½ POUNDS YUKON GOLD POTATOES (ABOUT 3 MEDIUM), PEELED AND THINLY SLICED

3   OUNCES GRUYÈRE CHEESE, SHREDDED (¾ CUP)

1 Preheat oven to 350°F. Grease shallow 4-cup baking dish or 9-inch glass pie plate. Set aside.

2 In 3-quart saucepan, combine half-and-half, cayenne, and salt; heat to boiling over medium-high heat.

3 Add potatoes and cook 2 minutes or until half-and-half mixture thickens slightly, stirring gently with heat-safe spatula.

4 Transfer half of potato mixture to prepared baking dish; sprinkle evenly with half of Gruyère. Top with remaining potato mixture and Gruyère.

5 Bake 35 to 40 minutes or until potatoes are fork-tender and top is golden and bubbly.

EACH SERVING: ABOUT 295 CALORIES | 11G PROTEIN | 33G CARBOHYDRATE | 14G TOTAL FAT (8G SATURATED) | 2G FIBER | 45MG CHOLESTEROL | 395MG SODIUM

OVEN FRITES

These crispy oven-baked fries are made with only one tablespoon of heart-healthy olive oil, making them low-fat as well as delicious. For photo, see page 104. For a change, try this method with sweet potatoes.

ACTIVE TIME: 10 MINUTES · **TOTAL TIME:** 45 MINUTES

MAKES: 4 SIDE-DISH SERVINGS

4	LARGE BAKING POTATOES (8 OUNCES EACH), NOT PEELED	¾	TEASPOON KOSHER SALT
1	TABLESPOON OLIVE OIL	¼	TEASPOON GROUND BLACK PEPPER

1 Preheat oven to 450°F. Scrub potatoes well; pat dry with paper towels.

2 Cut potatoes lengthwise into ½-inch-thick slices, then cut slices lengthwise into ½-inch-wide sticks.

3 Spray two 15½" by 10½" jelly-roll pans with nonstick cooking spray. In one pan, carefully toss all of potatoes with oil, salt, and pepper. Transfer half of potatoes to second jelly-roll pan.

4 Bake potatoes on two oven racks 30 to 35 minutes or until browned and crisp, rotating pans between upper and lower racks and stirring potatoes once halfway through cooking.

EACH SERVING: ABOUT 220 CALORIES | 4G PROTEIN | 44G CARBOHYDRATE | 4G TOTAL FAT (1G SATURATED) | 4G FIBER | 0MG CHOLESTEROL | 375MG SODIUM

CORN ON THE COB WITH MOLASSES BUTTER

Sink your teeth into this grilled corn topped off with a molasses-sweetened butter. Cayenne pepper and coriander add a little kick.

ACTIVE TIME: 10 MINUTES · **TOTAL TIME:** 20 MINUTES
MAKES: 8 SIDE-DISH SERVINGS

---

2   TABLESPOON BUTTER OR MARGARINE, SOFTENED

1   TEASPOON LIGHT (MILD) MOLASSES

½   TEASPOON GROUND CORIANDER

½   TEASPOON SALT

PINCH CAYENNE (GROUND RED) PEPPER

8   EARS CORN, HUSKS AND SILK REMOVED

1   Prepare outdoor grill for covered direct grilling over medium-high heat.
2   In small bowl, with fork, stir butter, molasses, coriander, salt, and cayenne until well combined.
3   Place corn on hot grill rack over medium-high heat. Cover grill and cook corn, turning frequently, until brown in spots, 10 to 15 minutes.
4   Transfer corn to platter; spread each ear with molasses butter.

EACH SERVING: ABOUT 105 CALORIES | 3G PROTEIN | 18G CARBOHYDRATE | 4G TOTAL FAT (2G SATURATED) | 2G FIBER | 8MG CHOLESTEROL | 186MG SODIUM

VEGETABLE-HERB STUFFING

Here's a classic stuffing to enjoy on holidays or whenever you have the craving. You can toast the bread a day in advance; when the slices are cool, transfer them to a zip-tight plastic bag and store at room temperature.

ACTIVE TIME: 20 MINUTES · **TOTAL TIME:** 1 HOUR 40 MINUTES
MAKES: 12 CUPS

1½ LOAVES (16 OUNCES EACH) SLICED FIRM WHITE BREAD

1 TABLESPOON OLIVE OIL

2 MEDIUM CARROTS, FINELY CHOPPED

2 MEDIUM STALKS CELERY, FINELY CHOPPED

1 MEDIUM ONION (ABOUT 8 OUNCES), FINELY CHOPPED

½ CUP LOOSELY PACKED FRESH PARSLEY LEAVES, COARSELY CHOPPED

¾ TEASPOON POULTRY SEASONING

½ TEASPOON SALT

¼ TEASPOON GROUND BLACK PEPPER

2½ CUPS CHICKEN BROTH (TO MAKE HOMEMADE, SEE PAGE 17)

1 Preheat oven to 400°F. Grease shallow 3- to 3½-quart baking dish.

2 Arrange bread slices on 2 cookie sheets and toast in oven 16 to 17 minutes or until golden and dry, turning slices over halfway through toasting.

3 Meanwhile, in 12-inch nonstick skillet, heat oil over medium heat for 1 minute or until hot. Add carrots, celery, and onion and cook, stirring occasionally, until vegetables are tender and lightly browned, about 12 minutes.

4 Remove skillet from heat; stir in parsley, poultry seasoning, salt, and pepper.

5 With serrated knife, cut bread into ½-inch cubes, then place in very large bowl. Reset oven control to 325°F.

6 Add broth and vegetable mixture to bread in bowl and toss until bread is evenly moistened.

7 Spoon stuffing into prepared baking dish. Cover dish with foil and bake 30 minutes. Remove foil and bake 15 to 20 minutes longer or until heated through and lightly browned on top.

EACH ½-CUP SERVING: ABOUT 90 CALORIES | 3G PROTEIN | 16G CARBOHYDRATE | 2G TOTAL FAT (0G SATURATED) | 1G FIBER | 0MG CHOLESTEROL | 270 MG SODIUM

NEW GREEN BEAN CASSEROLE

You don't have to wait until the holidays to dig into this healthier version of everyone's favorite green beans. We switched to low-fat milk and reduced-sodium broth, traded canned french-fried onions for oven-fried ones, cutting the calories by 53, trimming the total fat by 8 grams, and dropping the sodium by 257 milligrams. Seconds, anyone?

ACTIVE TIME: 30 MINUTES · **TOTAL TIME:** 45 MINUTES
MAKES: 8 SIDE-DISH SERVINGS

OLIVE-OIL NONSTICK COOKING SPRAY

1   LARGE (12-OUNCE) ONION, CUT INTO ½-INCH-THICK SLICES AND SEPARATED INTO RINGS

5   TABLESPOONS ALL-PURPOSE FLOUR

⅝   TEASPOON SALT

1½ POUNDS GREEN BEANS, TRIMMED

1   TABLESPOON BUTTER OR TRANS-FAT-FREE MARGARINE

1   LARGE SHALLOT, FINELY CHOPPED

1   (10-OUNCE) CONTAINER SLICED CREMINI OR WHITE MUSHROOMS

¼   TEASPOON GROUND BLACK PEPPER

1   CUP REDUCED-SODIUM CHICKEN BROTH

½   CUP LOW-FAT (1%) MILK

1 Preheat oven to 425°F. Line large cookie sheet with foil; spray with nonstick spray. In bowl, toss onion with 2 tablespoons flour and ⅛ teaspoon salt. Spread onion in single layer on prepared foil; spray onion with nonstick spray. Bake 14 minutes; toss to rearrange, then spray again. Bake 15 minutes or until crisp.

2 Meanwhile, in 5-quart saucepot, heat *3 quarts water* to boiling on high. Add beans and cook, uncovered, 5 minutes or until tender-crisp. Drain beans in colander; rinse under cold water. Drain.

3 In 4-quart saucepan, melt butter or margarine on medium. Add shallot; cook 2 minutes, stirring. Add mushrooms; cook 7 to 8 minutes or until tender, stirring often. Stir in ½ teaspoon salt, ¼ teaspoon pepper, and remaining 3 tablespoons flour; cook 1 minute. Add broth and milk; heat to boiling on high, stirring. Reduce heat to low; cook 2 minutes. Add beans.

4 Transfer mixture to 2-quart baking dish; bake 15 minutes. Stir mixture; top with onion. Bake 5 minutes or until sauce is bubbly.

EACH SERVING: ABOUT 95 CALORIES | 5G PROTEIN | 16G CARBOHYDRATE | 2G TOTAL FAT (0G SATURATED) | 4G FIBER | 1MG CHOLESTEROL | 285MG SODIUM

CREAMED SPINACH

Even those who swear they hate spinach may be seduced by this mild and creamy dish. For spinach lovers, it's heaven by the spoonful.

ACTIVE TIME: 20 MINUTES · **TOTAL TIME:** 35 MINUTES
MAKES: 6 SIDE-DISH SERVINGS

2   TABLESPOONS BUTTER OR MARGARINE

3   LARGE SHALLOTS, FINELY CHOPPED (ABOUT ¾ CUP)

2   TABLESPOONS ALL-PURPOSE FLOUR

½   CUP MILK

¾   TEASPOON SALT

¼   TEASPOON COARSELY GROUND BLACK PEPPER

⅛   TEASPOON NUTMEG

1   SMALL PACKAGE (3 OUNCES) CREAM CHEESE, SOFTENED AND CUT INTO PIECES

3   PACKAGES (10 OUNCES EACH) FROZEN CHOPPED SPINACH, THAWED AND SQUEEZED DRY

1   CUP LOOSELY PACKED FRESH PARSLEY LEAVES

¼   CUP SOUR CREAM

1 In 4-quart saucepan, melt butter over medium-low heat. Add shallots and cook, stirring frequently, until tender, about 3 minutes. Add flour and cook, stirring, 1 minute. With wire whisk, gradually whisk in milk; heat to boiling, whisking constantly. Reduce heat and simmer, stirring occasionally with wooden spoon until sauce has thickened and boils, about 2 minutes. Stir in salt, pepper, and nutmeg.

2 Remove from heat; stir in cream cheese until smooth. Stir in spinach, parsley, and sour cream; heat through, stirring frequently (do not boil).

EACH SERVING: ABOUT 180 CALORIES | 7G PROTEIN | 14G CARBOHYDRATE | 12G TOTAL FAT (7G SATURATED) | 33MG CHOLESTEROL | 500 MG SODIUM

POTATO LATKES WITH APPLESAUCE

These warm, crispy pancakes are a Hanukkah tradition. Using a food processor to chop the onion and potatoes makes assembly easy.

ACTIVE TIME: 15 MINUTES · **TOTAL TIME:** 55 MINUTES

MAKES: ABOUT 16 LATKES

---

3   TABLESPOONS ALL-PURPOSE FLOUR

1   TEASPOON SALT

½   TEASPOON BAKING POWDER

¼   TEASPOON GROUND BLACK PEPPER

1   MEDIUM ONION, GRATED

1   LARGE EGG, BEATEN

4   MEDIUM BAKING POTATOES (ABOUT 2½ POUNDS), PEELED AND CUT INTO 1-INCH PIECES

½   CUP VEGETABLE OIL

APPLESAUCE (TO MAKE HOMEMADE, SEE OPPOSITE)

1   Preheat oven to 250°F. Line a large cookie sheet with several layers of paper towels.

2   In large bowl, combine flour, salt, baking powder, pepper, onion, and egg.

3   In food processor with knife blade attached, process potatoes until finely chopped. Transfer potatoes to colander in sink and drain well. Stir potatoes into onion mixture in bowl until blended.

4   In nonstick 12-inch skillet, heat 2 tablespoons oil over medium heat until hot. With large serving spoon, drop about ¼ cup potato mixture into skillet; flatten into 4" by 3" oval. Repeat to make 3 more latkes.

5   Cook latkes 8 to 10 minutes or until browned on both sides, turning over once. (Reduce heat if browning too quickly.) With slotted spatula, transfer to lined cookie sheet to drain. Top with layer of paper towels, then cover loosely with foil. Keep warm in oven.

6   Repeat with remaining potato mixture, stirring mixture each time before frying and adding more oil to skillet as needed. Serve with applesauce.

EACH LATKE: ABOUT 150 CALORIES | 2G PROTEIN | 30G CARBOHYDRATE | 3G TOTAL FAT (0G SATURATED) | 1G FIBER | 1MG CHOLESTEROL | 165MG SODIUM

HOMEMADE APPLESAUCE

Peel and core **4 large Golden Delicious apples** (2 pounds); cut each into eighths. In 3-quart saucepan, combine apples, **½ cup apple cider or juice, ¼ cup sugar**, and **1 teaspoon fresh lemon juice**. Heat to boiling over high heat. Reduce heat to low; cover and simmer until apples are very tender, 20 to 25 minutes. Remove from heat; with potato masher, coarsely mash apples. Makes 3 cups.

EACH ½ CUP: ABOUT 70 CALORIES | 0G PROTEIN | 18G CARBOHYDRATE | 0G TOTAL FAT (0G SATURATED) | 0MG CHOLESTEROL | 0MG SODIUM

BREAKFASTS & BRUNCHES

Good morning! Here are delicious ways to make even weekdays special for grown-ups and kids alike. If eggs are the first thing that come to mind when you hear "breakfast," you'll welcome our easy, cheesy, omelet, a plate of huevos rancheros, or our brunch-worthy egg pies.

If something sweet is your idea of morning comfort food, you'll appreciate our slimmed-down French toast (we lighten it up with egg whites and low-fat milk). Or sink your teeth into our old-fashioned coffee cake—complete with streusel and a luscious glaze—or our cinnamon-sugar sconuts—a yummy cross between a scone and a doughnut.

Crustless Tomato-Ricotta Pie (see recipe page 125)

HUEVOS RANCHEROS

Featuring a medley of Mexican seasonings, black beans, and eggs over easy, our Huevos Rancheros bring the flavor (and the fiber) without the fat.

ACTIVE TIME: 5 MINUTES · TOTAL TIME: 25 MINUTES
MAKES: 4 MAIN-DISH SERVINGS

1	TABLESPOON VEGETABLE OIL	1	CAN (15 TO 19 OUNCES) BLACK BEANS, RINSED AND DRAINED
1	MEDIUM ONION, FINELY CHOPPED		
2	GARLIC CLOVES, CRUSHED WITH GARLIC PRESS	¼	CUP LOOSELY PACKED FRESH CILANTRO LEAVES, CHOPPED
1	TABLESPOON CHIPOTLE SAUCE OR OTHER HOT SAUCE, PLUS ADDITIONAL FOR SERVING	¼	TEASPOON SALT
		1	TABLESPOON BUTTER OR MARGARINE
1	TEASPOON GROUND CUMIN	4	LARGE EGGS
1	CAN (28 OUNCES) WHOLE TOMATOES IN JUICE, DRAINED AND CHOPPED (SEE TIP)	4	(6-INCH) CORN TORTILLAS, WARMED
		1	AVOCADO, SLICED (OPTIONAL)

1 In 4-quart saucepan, heat oil over medium heat until hot. Add onion and garlic and cook 8 minutes or until beginning to brown. Stir in chipotle sauce and cumin; cook 30 seconds, stirring. Add tomatoes.

2 Cover and cook 3 minutes to blend flavors, stirring occasionally. Stir in beans, half of cilantro, and salt; heat through, about 3 minutes, stirring occasionally.

3 Meanwhile, in nonstick 12-inch skillet, melt butter over medium heat. Crack eggs, 1 at a time, and drop into skillet. Cover skillet and cook eggs 4 to 5 minutes or until whites are set and yolks thicken.

4 Place tortillas on 4 dinner plates; top each with some tomato mixture and 1 egg. Sprinkle with remaining cilantro. Serve with sliced avocado and additional hot sauce, if desired.

TIP To avoid a mess on the cutting board and counter, "chop" the tomatoes right in the can using kitchen shears.

EACH SERVING: ABOUT 315 CALORIES | 15G PROTEIN | 42G CARBOHYDRATE | 12G TOTAL FAT (3G SATURATED) | 10G FIBER | 213MG CHOLESTEROL | 765MG SODIUM

CLASSIC CHEESE OMELET

Here's a classic omelet recipe to fill with your choice of shredded cheese. Because cooking time is so short, you'll need to have your eggs, seasonings, and fillings at your elbow so you can give individual attention to each omelet. A side of toast—and, depending on the time of day, a glass of juice or wine—completes the meal.

ACTIVE TIME: 5 MINUTES · TOTAL TIME: 20 MINUTES
MAKES: 4 MAIN-DISH SERVINGS

8   LARGE EGGS

½   CUP WATER

½   TEASPOON SALT

½   TEASPOON GROUND BLACK PEPPER

2   TABLESPOONS BUTTER OR MARGARINE

4   OUNCES SHREDDED CHEDDAR, GRUYÈRE, OR FONTINA CHEESE (1 CUP)

CHOPPED GREEN ONIONS

TOASTED COUNTRY-STYLE BREAD (OPTIONAL)

1   Preheat oven to 200°F.

2   Place 4 dinner plates in oven to warm. In bowl, place eggs, water, salt, and pepper. With fork, beat 25 to 30 quick strokes to blend mixture without making it fluffy. (Overbeating eggs toughens proteins in whites.)

3   In nonstick 8-inch skillet, melt 1½ teaspoons butter over medium heat. When butter stops sizzling, pour or ladle ½ cup egg mixture into skillet.

4   After egg mixture begins to set around edges, about 25 to 30 seconds, with heat-safe spatula, carefully push cooked egg from side of skillet toward center, so uncooked egg can reach bottom of hot skillet. Repeat 8 to 10 times around skillet, tilting as necessary, 1 to 1½ minutes.

5   Cook until omelet is almost set but still creamy and moist on top. Place skillet handle facing you, and sprinkle ¼ cup cheese on half of omelet.

6   With spatula, fold omelet in half, covering cheese.

7   Shake pan gently to loosen any egg or cheese from edge, then slide omelet to edge of skillet.

8   Holding skillet above warm plate, tip skillet so omelet slides onto plate. Put plate in oven to keep omelet warm. Repeat with remaining butter, egg mixture, and cheese to make 4 omelets in all. Sprinkle with green onions. Serve with toast, if desired.

EACH SERVING: ABOUT 315 CALORIES | 20G PROTEIN | 2G CARBOHYDRATE | 25G TOTAL FAT (10G SATURATED) | 0G FIBER | 455MG CHOLESTEROL | 670MG SODIUM

CRUSTLESS TOMATO-RICOTTA PIE

This delicious cross between a frittata and a quiche makes a great vegetarian brunch or dinner option. For photo, see page 120.

ACTIVE TIME: 20 MINUTES · **TOTAL TIME:** 1 HOUR 15 MINUTES PLUS STANDING
MAKES: 6 MAIN-DISH SERVINGS

1 CONTAINER (15 OUNCES) PART-SKIM RICOTTA CHEESE	1 TABLESPOON CORNSTARCH
4 LARGE EGGS	½ CUP LOOSELY PACKED FRESH BASIL LEAVES, CHOPPED
¼ CUP FRESHLY GRATED PECORINO-ROMANO CHEESE	½ CUP LOOSELY PACKED FRESH MINT LEAVES, CHOPPED
½ TEASPOON SALT	1 POUND RIPE TOMATOES (ABOUT 3 MEDIUM), THINLY SLICED
⅛ TEASPOON COARSELY GROUND BLACK PEPPER	
¼ CUP LOW-FAT MILK (1%)	

1 Preheat oven to 375°F. In large bowl, whisk ricotta, eggs, Pecorino, salt, and pepper until blended.

2 In measuring cup, stir milk and cornstarch until smooth; whisk into cheese mixture. Stir in basil and mint.

3 Pour mixture into nonstick 10-inch skillet with oven-safe handle. Arrange tomatoes on top, overlapping slices if necessary. Bake pie 35 to 40 minutes or until lightly browned and set around edge and center is puffed. Let stand 5 minutes before serving.

TIP Flavorful variations: Substitute 2 tablespoons chopped fresh oregano or ¼ cup chopped fresh dill for the basil.

EACH SERVING: ABOUT 190 CALORIES | 15G PROTEIN | 10G CARBOHYDRATE | 10G TOTAL FAT (5G SATURATED) | 2G FIBER | 165MG CHOLESTEROL | 380MG SODIUM

FLORENTINE FRITTATA

This frittata is a cheesy wonder, combining the smooth creaminess of mozzarella and the salty tang of feta.

ACTIVE TIME: 10 MINUTES · **TOTAL TIME:** 20 MINUTES
MAKES: 4 MAIN-DISH SERVINGS

1 PACKAGE (10 OUNCES) FROZEN CHOPPED SPINACH, THAWED AND SQUEEZED DRY

4 LARGE EGGS

4 LARGE EGG WHITES

2 GREEN ONIONS, THINLY SLICED

¼ CUP CRUMBLED FETA CHEESE

¾ CUP SHREDDED PART-SKIM MOZZARELLA CHEESE (3 OUNCES)

¼ TEASPOON SALT

1 TABLESPOON OLIVE OIL

1 CUP GRAPE OR CHERRY TOMATOES

1 Preheat broiler. In large bowl, mix spinach, eggs, egg whites, green onions, feta, ½ cup mozzarella, and salt until well blended.

2 In broiler-safe 10-inch skillet, heat oil over medium heat. Pour egg mixture into skillet; arrange tomatoes on top, pushing some down. Cover skillet and cook 5 to 6 minutes or until egg mixture is just set around edge.

3 Place skillet in broiler 6 inches from source of heat and broil 4 to 5 minutes or until just set in center. Sprinkle with remaining mozzarella; broil about 1 minute longer or until cheese melts.

4 To serve, loosen frittata from skillet and cut into wedges.

EACH SERVING: ABOUT 230 CALORIES | 18G PROTEIN | 6G CARBOHYDRATE | 14G TOTAL FAT (6G SATURATED) | 2G FIBER | 233MG CHOLESTEROL | 570MG SODIUM

HAM AND PEPPER-JACK SOUFFLÉ

Ham and pepper Jack cheese partner up in this light and fluffy soufflé that can be served for brunch or dinner with a simple green salad.

ACTIVE TIME: 20 MINUTES · TOTAL TIME: 1 HOUR 20 MINUTES

MAKES: 6 MAIN-DISH SERVINGS

---

4   TABLESPOONS BUTTER OR MARGARINE

¼   CUP ALL-PURPOSE FLOUR

1½ CUPS REDUCED-FAT MILK (2%), WARMED

6   OUNCES PEPPER JACK CHEESE, SHREDDED (1½ CUPS)

4   LARGE EGGS, SEPARATED

1   LARGE EGG WHITE

3   OUNCES SMOKED HAM, CHOPPED (½ CUP)

1   CAN (4½ OUNCES) CHOPPED MILD GREEN CHILES, DRAINED

1 Preheat oven to 325°F. Grease 2-quart soufflé dish.

2 In heavy 2-quart saucepan, melt butter over low heat. Add flour and cook 1 minute, stirring. With wire whisk, gradually mix in milk. Cook over medium heat, stirring constantly, until sauce thickens and boils.

3 Reduce heat to low and simmer 3 minutes, stirring frequently. Stir in Pepper Jack and cook, stirring constantly, just until cheese melts and sauce is smooth. Remove saucepan from heat.

4 In medium bowl, with whisk, lightly beat egg yolks; gradually whisk in hot cheese sauce. Stir in ham and chiles.

5 In large bowl, with mixer on high speed, beat 5 egg whites until stiff peaks form when beaters are lifted. With rubber spatula, gently fold one-third of beaten egg whites into cheese mixture. Fold in remaining whites just until blended.

6 Pour mixture into prepared soufflé dish. Bake about 50 minutes or until soufflé is puffed and golden brown and knife inserted 1 inch from edge comes out clean. Serve immediately.

EACH SERVING: ABOUT 295 CALORIES | 17G PROTEIN | 9G CARBOHYDRATE | 22G TOTAL FAT (9G SATURATED) | 1G FIBER | 183MG CHOLESTEROL | 595MG SODIUM

FAVORITE FRENCH TOAST

Our slimmed-down take on this Sunday-morning favorite is practically saintly but oh-so-good. Subbing in low-fat milk and egg whites gives it half the fat and a third less cholesterol than traditional French toast—allowing you to enjoy your maple syrup without guilt.

ACTIVE TIME: 5 MINUTES · TOTAL TIME: 20 MINUTES
MAKES: 4 MAIN-DISH SERVINGS

---

2   LARGE EGG WHITES

1   LARGE EGG

¾   CUP LOW-FAT (1%) MILK

¼   TEASPOON VANILLA EXTRACT

⅛   TEASPOON SALT

2   TEASPOONS BUTTER OR MARGARINE

8   SLICES FIRM WHOLE-WHEAT BREAD

MAPLE SYRUP AND FRESH BERRIES (OPTIONAL)

1   Preheat oven to 200°F. In pie plate, with whisk, beat egg whites, egg, milk, vanilla extract, and salt until blended. In nonstick 12-inch skillet, melt 1 teaspoon butter over medium heat.

2   Dip bread slices, 1 at a time, in egg mixture, pressing bread lightly to coat both sides well. Place 3 or 4 slices in skillet, and, turning once, cook 6 to 8 minutes or until lightly browned.

3   Transfer French toast to cookie sheet; keep warm in oven. Repeat with remaining butter, bread slices, and egg mixture. Serve French toast with maple syrup and berries, if you like.

EACH SERVING: ABOUT 300 CALORIES | 12G PROTEIN | 46G CARBOHYDRATE | 9G TOTAL FAT (2G SATURATED) | 6G FIBER | 56MG CHOLESTEROL | 7MG SODIUM

STREUSEL COFFEE CAKE

This old-fashioned coffee cake is sure to be a hit at any coffee klatch, potluck, or brunch buffet. A ribbon of cinnamon-sugar sprinkled pecans winds through the center of this cake. Sour cream makes it extra moist; a luscious vanilla glaze makes it completely irresistible, though you could skip the glaze if you prefer and simply sprinkle the cake with a little confectioners' sugar.

ACTIVE TIME: 30 MINUTES · **TOTAL TIME:** 1 HOUR 30 MINUTES PLUS COOLING
MAKES: 16 SERVINGS

1½ TEASPOONS BAKING POWDER

1 TEASPOON BAKING SODA

¾ TEASPOON SALT

3 CUPS PLUS 1 TABLESPOON ALL-PURPOSE FLOUR

¾ CUP CHOPPED PECANS

⅓ CUP PACKED BROWN SUGAR

1¼ TEASPOONS GROUND CINNAMON

1½ CUPS GRANULATED SUGAR

¾ CUP BUTTER OR MARGARINE (1½ STICKS), SOFTENED

2½ TEASPOONS VANILLA EXTRACT

3 LARGE EGGS

2 CONTAINERS (8 OUNCES EACH) SOUR CREAM

1 CUP CONFECTIONERS' SUGAR

4 TO 6 TEASPOONS MILK

1 Preheat oven to 350°F. Grease 12-cup fluted bundt pan (see Tip, opposite); dust with flour.

2 On waxed paper, combine baking powder, baking soda, salt, and 3 cups flour. In small bowl, combine pecans, brown sugar, cinnamon, and remaining 1 tablespoon flour.

3 In large bowl, with mixer on medium speed, beat granulated sugar, butter, and 2 teaspoons vanilla until creamy. Beat in eggs 1 at a time. Alternately beat in flour mixture and sour cream; start and end with flour mixture. Beat just until blended, occasionally scraping bowl with spatula.

4 Spread 2 cups batter in bottom of prepared pan; sprinkle with half of nut mixture. Top with 2 cups batter; gently spread with spatula to cover nut mixture, being careful not to lift nut mixture out of place. Sprinkle batter with remaining nut mixture, then spread with remaining batter.

5 Bake 60 minutes or until toothpick inserted in center comes out clean. Cool in pan on rack 10 minutes. With spatula, loosen cake from pan. Invert cake onto rack; remove pan and cool completely.

6   Prepare glaze: In bowl, stir confectioners' sugar, milk, and remaining ½ teaspoon vanilla until smooth. Transfer cake to plate; with spoon, drizzle glaze over cake. Let glaze set 15 minutes before serving.

TIP European baking traditions are echoed in the Bundt pan, a large, deeply fluted tube pan. Choose a good-quality pan made from heavy-duty aluminum with well-sealed seams (if any) and nicely rounded edges. A nonstick surface makes cakes easier to remove. Bundt cake recipes, including this one, can also be baked in two 9" by 5" loaf pans; remove the cakes from the pan before drizzling with glaze.

EACH SERVING: ABOUT 410 CALORIES | 5G PROTEIN | 51G CARBOHYDRATE | 21G TOTAL FAT (10G SATURATED) | 1G FIBER | 77MG CHOLESTEROL | 550MG SODIUM

OATMEAL SCONUTS

Sconuts, a riff on two breakfast favorites, are pumped full of oats with a hint of nutmeg to mimic the cake doughnuts found at the farmer's market.

ACTIVE TIME: 10 MINUTES · TOTAL TIME: 25 MINUTES

MAKES: 13 SCONUTS

2 CUPS OLD-FASHIONED ROLLED OATS

2 CUPS ALL-PURPOSE FLOUR

½ CUP BROWN SUGAR

2½ TEASPOONS BAKING POWDER

½ TEASPOON BAKING SODA

½ TEASPOON SALT

¼ TEASPOON GROUND NUTMEG

½ CUP BUTTER (1 STICK), CUT INTO PIECES

¾ CUP BUTTERMILK

1 LARGE EGG

CINNAMON-SUGAR

1 Preheat oven to 425°F.

2 In food processor with knife-blade attached, combine oats, flour, brown sugar, baking powder, baking soda, salt, and nutmeg; pulse to blend. Add butter; pulse until coarse crumbs form.

3 In cup, beat buttermilk and egg. With processor running, add egg mixture and pulse until a dough forms.

4 Scoop dough by ¼ cups onto ungreased large cookie sheet. Flatten each mound into a 2½-inch round. Sprinkle with cinnamon-sugar. Bake 15 minutes or until golden on bottoms.

TIP Pop extras into a zip-tight bag and freeze for up to one month (to warm, microwave for about twenty seconds).

EACH SCONUT: ABOUT 235 CALORIES | 5G PROTEIN | 34G CARBOHYDRATE | 9G TOTAL FAT (5G SATURATED) | 2G FIBER | 37MG CHOLESTEROL | 315MG SODIUM

FAVORITE DESSERTS

These sinfully delicious cakes, cookies, pies, and puddings are all perfect endings to memorable meals. If chocolate is your comfort food of choice, you're in luck: We have scrumptious recipes for chocolate-chip brownies, a classic layer cake, and a dark chocolate pie with a caramel-walnut swirl. Cheesecake lovers can select their bliss—either lemon ricotta with a graham-cracker crust or milk chocolate with a chocolate-wafer crust.

If you need a quick pick-me-up, sink your teeth into one of our oatmeal-raisin cookies, studded with chocolate chips, if you choose. Our hot cocoa will also do the job: In addition to the classic chocolate, we offer vanilla, mocha, and Mexican-chocolate flavor variations.

Milk Chocolate Cheesecake (recipe page 147)

COCOA BROWNIES WITH MINI CHOCOLATE CHIPS

Rich cocoa brownies studded with mini chocolate chips figure prominently in our vision of comfort food. We like to cool them completely before serving because they are sometimes too soft to cut when warm.

ACTIVE TIME: 15 MINUTES · **TOTAL TIME:** 35 MINUTES PLUS COOLING
MAKES: 16 BROWNIES

½ CUP ALL-PURPOSE FLOUR

½ CUP UNSWEETENED COCOA

¼ TEASPOON BAKING POWDER

¼ TEASPOON SALT

6 TABLESPOONS BUTTER OR MARGARINE

1 CUP SUGAR

2 LARGE EGGS

2 TEASPOONS VANILLA EXTRACT

⅓ CUP MINI CHOCOLATE CHIPS

1 Preheat oven to 350°F. Grease 8-inch square baking pan. On waxed paper, combine flour, cocoa, baking powder, and salt.

2 In 3-quart saucepan, melt butter over low heat. Remove from heat; with rubber spatula, stir in sugar, then eggs, 1 at a time, and vanilla until well blended. Stir in flour mixture. Spread batter in prepared pan; sprinkle with chocolate chips.

3 Bake 18 to 20 minutes or until toothpick inserted 2 inches from center comes out almost clean. Cool brownies completely in pan on wire rack, about 2 hours.

4 When completely cool, cut brownies into 4 strips, then cut each strip crosswise into 4 squares.

EACH BROWNIE: ABOUT 120 CALORIES | 2G PROTEIN | 17G CARBOHYDRATE | 6G TOTAL FAT (3G SATURATED) | 1G FIBER | 39MG CHOLESTEROL | 100MG SODIUM

CHEWY OATMEAL-RAISIN COOKIES

Who can resist a plate of homemade raisin-studded oatmeal cookies? Or for a luxurious take on this classic cookie, swap in tart dried cherries and chocolate chips instead of the raisins.

ACTIVE TIME: 45 MINUTES · TOTAL TIME: 1 HOUR 45 MINUTES
MAKES: ABOUT 54 COOKIES

1½ CUPS ALL-PURPOSE FLOUR

2 TEASPOONS BAKING SODA

½ TEASPOON SALT

¾ CUPS GRANULATED SUGAR

¾ CUPS PACKED BROWN SUGAR

¾ CUPS BUTTER OR MARGARINE (1½ STICKS), SOFTENED

2 LARGE EGGS

2 TEASPOONS VANILLA EXTRACT

3 CUPS OLD-FASHIONED OATS, UNCOOKED

1 CUP RAISINS OR DRIED CHERRIES

1 PACKAGE (6 OUNCES) SEMI-SWEET CHOCOLATE CHIPS (OPTIONAL)

1   Preheat oven to 350°F. Grease two large cookie sheets. In small bowl, with wire whisk, stir flour, baking soda, and salt until blended.

2   In large bowl, with mixer at medium speed, beat granulated and brown sugars and butter until creamy, occasionally scraping bowl with rubber spatula. Beat in eggs, one at a time, beating well after each addition. Beat in vanilla. Reduce speed to low; gradually beat in flour mixture just until blended, occasionally scraping bowl.

3   With wooden spoon, stir in oats, raisins, and chocolate chips, if using, until well combined.

4   Drop dough by rounded tablespoons, 2 inches apart, onto prepared cookie sheets. Bake cookies until tops are golden, 12 to 14 minutes (see Tip), rotating cookie sheets between upper and lower racks halfway through baking. With wide spatula, transfer cookies to wire racks to cool Repeat with any remaining dough.

TIP For chewy cookies, bake the minimum time; for crispy cookies, bake a few minutes longer.

EACH COOKIE: ABOUT 90 CALORIES | 1G PROTEIN | 4G CARBOHYDRATE | 3G TOTAL FAT (2G SATURATED) | 1G FIBER | 15MG CHOLESTEROL | 90MG SODIUM

DARK CHOCOLATE– WALNUT CARAMEL PIE

This decadent pie, made with dark chocolate, creamy homemade caramel, and toasted walnuts, is well worth the calorie splurge.

ACTIVE TIME: 25 MINUTES · **TOTAL TIME:** 1 HOUR 5 MINUTES PLUS COOLING
MAKES: 12 SERVINGS

- 1 (9-INCH) FROZEN DEEP-DISH PIE SHELL
- 1 CUP SUGAR
- ¼ CUP WATER
- 1¼ CUPS HEAVY OR WHIPPING CREAM
- 8 OUNCES SEMISWEET CHOCOLATE, CUT INTO PIECES
- 2 TABLESPOONS BUTTER OR MARGARINE
- 2 TEASPOONS VANILLA EXTRACT
- 1¾ CUPS WALNUTS, TOASTED AND COARSELY CHOPPED

1   Thaw and bake pie shell according to package directions. Let stand until cool, at least 15 minutes.

2   In heavy 3-quart saucepan, heat sugar and water over medium-high heat until sugar dissolves and turns amber in color, 15 minutes, swirling pan occasionally.

3   Meanwhile, in microwave-safe 1-cup liquid measuring cup, heat ¾ cup cream in microwave on High 45 seconds or until warm. Reserve remaining ½ cup cream in refrigerator to keep cold for whipping later.

4   Remove saucepan from heat. Stir in warm cream until a smooth caramel forms (caramel will stiffen when cream is added). Stir in chocolate and butter until completely melted. Stir in vanilla and 1½ cups walnuts.

5   Pour warm chocolate filling into pie shell. Cool 1 hour on wire rack, then cover and refrigerate until set, at least 3 hours.

6   When ready to serve, in medium bowl, with mixer on medium speed, beat remaining ½ cup cream until soft peaks form. With metal spatula, spread whipped cream on top of pie, leaving ½-inch border all around. Sprinkle with reserved walnuts.

EACH SERVING: ABOUT 500 CALORIES | 6G PROTEIN | 40G CARBOHYDRATE | 37G TOTAL FAT (15G SATURATED) | 3G FIBER | 53MG CHOLESTEROL | 130MG SODIUM

EASIEST-EVER APPLE PIE

We'll never tell! Store-bought piecrust and a filling precooked in the microwave make this pie fast and easy—and absolutely delicious!

ACTIVE TIME: 10 MINUTES · TOTAL TIME: 35 MINUTES PLUS COOLING
MAKES: 10 SERVINGS

1 FROZEN DEEP-DISH PIE SHELL (SEE TIP)

½ CUP CHOPPED PECANS

¼ CUP ALL-PURPOSE FLOUR

¼ CUP PACKED BROWN SUGAR

2 TABLESPOONS BUTTER OR MARGARINE

1 LARGE EGG WHITE

¼ CUP GRANULATED SUGAR

2 TABLESPOONS CORNSTARCH

½ TEASPOON GROUND CINNAMON

3 POUNDS GRANNY SMITH, GOLDEN DELICIOUS, AND/OR GALA APPLES, CORED AND PEELED, EACH CUT INTO 8 WEDGES

1 TABLESPOON FRESH LEMON JUICE

VANILLA ICE CREAM (OPTIONAL)

1 Preheat oven to 375°F. While crust thaws at room temperature 15 minutes, mix pecans, flour, and brown sugar in bowl. Work in butter with fingertips until mixture resembles coarse crumbs. Set aside.

2 Prick bottom and sides of crust with fork. Bake 12 to 15 minutes or until lightly golden. Immediately brush bottom and sides of hot crust with light coating of egg white. Reset oven control to 425°F.

3 Meanwhile, in large bowl, combine granulated sugar, cornstarch, and cinnamon. Toss in apples and lemon juice. Cover with waxed paper and microwave on high 12 minutes, stirring halfway through.

4 Spoon filling into pie shell. Sprinkle pecan topping over filling.

5 Bake pie 10 to 12 minutes or until topping is golden. Cool on wire rack. Serve with vanilla ice cream, if you like.

TIP For a looks-like-homemade presentation, use our trick to transfer the store-bought crust from its foil pan to a 9-inch pie plate: Gently fold back foil around edge of frozen crust and pull slightly on the crust to remove from foil. Transfer to pie plate and thaw as directed. With fingertips, press lightly on thawed dough to mold into shape of pie plate.

EACH SERVING: ABOUT 290 CALORIES | 3G PROTEIN | 43G CARBOHYDRATE | 12G TOTAL FAT (3G SATURATED) | 3G FIBER | 7MG CHOLESTEROL | 120MG SODIUM

LEMON RICOTTA CHEESECAKE

A luscious lemon cheesecake with a cookie-crumb crust. For photo, see page 6.

ACTIVE TIME: 30 MINUTES · TOTAL TIME: 1 HOUR 45 MINUTES PLUS CHILLING

MAKES: 16 SERVINGS

- 1 CUP GRAHAM CRACKER CRUMBS
- 4 TABLESPOONS BUTTER OR MARGARINE, SOFTENED
- 3 TO 4 LEMONS
- 1¼ CUPS SUGAR
- ¼ CUP CORNSTARCH
- 2 PACKAGES (8 OUNCES EACH) REDUCED-FAT CREAM CHEESE (NEUFCHÂTEL), SOFTENED

- 1 CONTAINER (15 OUNCES) PART-SKIM RICOTTA CHEESE
- 4 LARGE EGGS
- 2 CUPS HALF-AND-HALF OR LIGHT CREAM
- 2 TEASPOONS VANILLA EXTRACT

1   Preheat oven to 375°F. Wrap outside of 9-inch springform pan with heavy-duty foil to prevent batter leaking.

2   In pan, mix graham cracker crumbs and butter, with fork, until crumbs are moistened. With hand, press mixture firmly onto bottom of pan. Bake crust 10 minutes. Cool on wire rack about 15 minutes.

3   Reset oven control to 325°F. From 2 lemons, grate 2 teaspoons peel and squeeze ⅓ cup juice. In small bowl, stir together sugar and cornstarch until blended. In large bowl, with mixer on medium speed, beat cream cheese and ricotta until smooth, about 5 minutes. Slowly beat in sugar mixture. Reduce speed to low; beat in eggs, half-and-half, vanilla, and lemon peel and juice just until blended, scraping bowl often with rubber spatula.

4   Pour batter onto crust. Bake 1 hour. Turn off oven; let cheesecake remain in oven 1 hour.

5   Remove cake from oven. To help prevent cracking as cake cools, run a knife between edge of cake and pan. Cool cake in pan on wire rack 2 hours. Cover and refrigerate until well chilled, at least 6 hours.

6   To serve, remove foil and side of pan and place cheesecake on plate. Cut 8 very thin lemon slices for garnish. To slice, see Tip, opposite.

EACH SERVING: ABOUT 300 CALORIES | 9G PROTEIN | 26G CARBOHYDRATE | 18G TOTAL FAT (10G SATURATED) | 0G FIBER | 102MG CHOLESTEROL | 235MG SODIUM

MILK CHOCOLATE CHEESECAKE

How to make the classic cheesecake even creamier? Add milk chocolate with a dark cookie crust for kicks. For photo, see page 136.

ACTIVE TIME: 25 MINUTES · TOTAL TIME: 1 HOUR 25 MINUTES PLUS CHILLING
MAKES: 20 SERVINGS

9 OUNCES (ONE-HALF PACKAGE) CHOCOLATE WAFER COOKIES

6 TABLESPOONS BUTTER OR MARGARINE, MELTED

2 PACKAGES (8 OUNCES EACH) CREAM CHEESE, SOFTENED

½ CUP PLUS 2 TABLESPOONS SUGAR

¼ TEASPOON SALT

3 LARGE EGGS, LIGHTLY BEATEN

¼ CUP WHOLE MILK

2 TEASPOONS VANILLA EXTRACT

1 PACKAGE (11½ OUNCES) MILK CHOCOLATE CHIPS, MELTED

1½ CUPS SOUR CREAM

1 Preheat oven to 350°F. In food processor with knife blade attached, pulse cookies until fine crumbs form. Add butter to crumbs and pulse several times to combine. Transfer cookie mixture to 9-inch springform pan; press onto bottom and about 2 inches up side of pan to form crust. Bake crust 10 minutes. Cool completely in pan on wire rack.

2 In large bowl, with mixer on medium speed, beat cream cheese, ½ cup sugar, and salt 2 minutes or until smooth, occasionally scraping bowl with rubber spatula. Reduce speed to low. Add eggs, milk, and vanilla and beat just until blended. Add chocolate and beat until combined.

3 Pour cream-cheese mixture into crust. Bake cheesecake 45 minutes (cake will jiggle slightly in center). Meanwhile, in small bowl, stir sour cream and remaining 2 tablespoons sugar until sugar dissolves; set aside.

4 Remove cheesecake from oven. Gently spread sour-cream mixture on top. Return cake to oven and bake 5 minutes longer to set sour cream.

5 Remove cheesecake from oven and cool completely in pan on wire rack. Cover and refrigerate at least 6 hours until well chilled, or up to 3 days.

TIP For perfect servings of cheesecake—that don't stick to your knife—dip knife into warm water and wipe dry before cutting each slice.

EACH SERVING: ABOUT 315 CALORIES | 5G PROTEIN | 27 G CARBOHYDRATE | 22G TOTAL FAT (12G SATURATED) | 0G FIBER | 74MG CHOLESTEROL | 755MG SODIUM

CHOCOLATE BUTTERMILK CAKE

This old-fashioned chocolatey layer cake is topped with swirls of luscious cream-cheese frosting.

ACTIVE TIME: 45 MINUTES · TOTAL TIME: 1 HOUR 15 MINUTES PLUS COOLING
MAKES: 16 SERVINGS

2	CUPS ALL-PURPOSE FLOUR	1¾	CUPS SUGAR
1	CUP UNSWEETENED COCOA	¾	CUP (1½ STICKS) BUTTER OR MARGARINE, SOFTENED
1½	TEASPOONS BAKING SODA		
¾	TEASPOON SALT	3	LARGE EGGS
1½	CUPS BUTTERMILK		VANILLA CREAM-CHEESE FROSTING (OPPOSITE)
2	TEASPOONS VANILLA EXTRACT		

1 Preheat oven to 350°F. Grease two 9-inch round cake pans. Line bottoms of pans with waxed paper. Grease waxed paper; dust with cocoa, shaking out excess.

2 On sheet of waxed paper, combine flour, cocoa, baking soda, and salt. In 2-cup liquid measuring cup, mix buttermilk and vanilla; set aside.

3 In bowl, with mixer on low speed, beat sugar and butter until blended. Increase speed to high; beat 3 minutes or until creamy, occasionally scraping bowl with spatula. Reduce speed to low; add eggs, 1 at a time, beating well after each addition.

4 Beat in flour mixture alternately with buttermilk mixture just until blended, beginning and ending with flour mixture, scraping bowl occasionally with rubber spatula.

5 Pour batter into prepared pans. Bake 30 to 35 minutes or until toothpick inserted in center of cake comes out clean. Cool in pans on wire racks 10 minutes. Invert cakes onto racks to cool completely. Carefully remove and discard waxed paper.

6 Prepare Vanilla Cream-Cheese Frosting.

7 Place 1 cake layer, rounded side down, on plate. With narrow spatula, spread ⅔ cup frosting over layer. Top with second layer, rounded side up. Spread remaining frosting over side and top of cake.

EACH SERVING: ABOUT 255 CALORIES | 5G PROTEIN | 37G CARBOHYDRATE | 11G TOTAL FAT (7G SATURATED) | 2G FIBER | 65MG CHOLESTEROL | 360MG SODIUM

VANILLA CREAM-CHEESE FROSTING

This creamy frosting also pairs beautifully with carrot cake.

TOTAL TIME: 10 MINUTES

MAKES: ABOUT 3½ CUPS

½ CUP BUTTER (1 STICK), SOFTENED (NO SUBSTITUTIONS)

8 OUNCES CREAM CHEESE, SOFTENED

2 TEASPOONS VANILLA EXTRACT

16 OUNCES CONFECTIONERS' SUGAR

1 In large bowl, with mixer at medium-high speed, beat butter, cream cheese, and vanilla 2 minutes or until light and fluffy. Reduce speed to low.
2 Beat in sugar until blended. Increase speed to medium-high; beat 2 minutes or until light and creamy.

EACH TABLESPOON: ABOUT 60 CALORIES | 0G PROTEIN | 8G CARBOHYDRATE | 3G TOTAL FAT (2G SATURATED) | 0G FIBER | 9MG CHOLESTEROL | 30MG SODIUM

VANILLA CRÈME BRÛLÉE

This classic baked custard gets a last-minute broil to create the crisp sugar crust. Crack with a spoon to dip into its sweet, creamy goodness.

ACTIVE TIME: 15 MINUTES · TOTAL TIME: 50 MINUTES PLUS COOLING AND CHILLING
MAKES: 6 SERVINGS

1 CUP LIGHT CREAM OR HALF-AND-HALF

1 CUP HEAVY OR WHIPPING CREAM

1½ TEASPOONS VANILLA EXTRACT

5 LARGE EGG YOLKS

⅓ CUP GRANULATED SUGAR

2 TABLESPOONS DARK BROWN SUGAR

1 Preheat oven to 325°F. Into 13" by 9" baking pan, pour 3½ cups hot water; place in oven.

2 In microwave-safe 2-cup liquid measuring cup, heat light and heavy creams in microwave on medium (50% power) 5 minutes. Remove from microwave; stir in vanilla.

3 Meanwhile, in 4-cup liquid measuring cup (to make pouring easier later) or bowl, whisk egg yolks and granulated sugar until well blended. Slowly whisk in warm cream mixture until combined; with spoon, skim off foam.

4 Partially pull out oven rack with baking pan. Place six 4-ounce ramekins in water in pan. Pour cream mixture into ramekins. (Mixture should come almost to tops of ramekins for successful broiling later.) Carefully push in rack and bake custards 30 minutes or until just set but centers jiggle slightly. Remove ramekins from water and place on wire rack; cool 30 minutes. Cover and refrigerate until well chilled, at least 4 hours or overnight.

5 At least 1 hour before serving, preheat broiler. Place brown sugar in coarse sieve; with spoon, press sugar through sieve to evenly cover tops of chilled custards. Place ramekins in jelly-roll pan for easier handling. With broiler rack at closest position to source of heat, broil custards 2 to 3 minutes or just until brown sugar melts. Refrigerate immediately 1 hour to cool custards and allow sugar to form a crust.

EACH SERVING: ABOUT 365 CALORIES | 4G PROTEIN | 18G CARBOHYDRATE | 31G TOTAL FAT (18G SATURATED) | 0G FIBER | 276MG CHOLESTEROL | 35MG SODIUM

RICE PUDDING

Cooking the rice very slowly in lots of milk makes this pudding especially creamy. Serve with fresh berries.

ACTIVE TIME: 10 MINUTES · TOTAL TIME: 1 HOUR 25 MINUTES
MAKES: 6 SERVINGS

4	CUPS MILK	¼	TEASPOON SALT
½	CUP REGULAR LONG-GRAIN RICE	1	LARGE EGG
½	CUP SUGAR	1	TEASPOON VANILLA EXTRACT

1   In heavy, 4-quart saucepan, combine milk, rice, sugar, and salt; heat to boiling over medium-high heat, stirring frequently. Reduce heat; cover and simmer mixture, stirring occasionally, until rice is very tender, about 1 hour.
2   In small bowl, with fork, lightly beat egg; stir in ½ cup hot rice mixture, stirring rapidly to prevent curdling. Cook, stirring constantly, until rice mixture has thickened, about 5 minutes (do not boil, or mixture will curdle).
3   Remove from heat; stir in vanilla. Serve warm or spoon into medium bowl and refrigerate until well chilled, about 3 hours.

EACH SERVING: ABOUT 235 CALORIES | 7G PROTEIN | 37G CARBOHYDRATE | 6G TOTAL FAT (4G SATURATED) | 58MG CHOLESTEROL | 187MG SODIUM

HOMEMADE HOT COCOA MIX

On a wintry day, hot chocolate is the ultimate comfort-in-a-cup, whether you're still a kid or just a kid at heart.

TOTAL TIME: 10 MINUTES

MAKES: 3½ CUPS MIX OR 18 SERVINGS COCOA

1½ CUPS UNSWEETENED COCOA

1¼ CUPS SUGAR

6 OUNCES SEMISWEET CHOCOLATE, COARSELY CHOPPED

¼ TEASPOON SALT

1 To make hot cocoa mix: In food processor, with knife blade attached, blend unsweetened cocoa, sugar, chocolate, and salt until almost smooth. Store in tightly sealed container at room temperature up to 6 months.

2 To make hot cocoa: For each serving, in a microwave-safe mug, mix 3 tablespoons cocoa mix with 1 cup milk. On High, microwave 1½ to 2 minutes or until blended and hot, stirring once. Top with a dollop of whipped cream.

EACH SERVING, DRY MIX ONLY: ABOUT 115 CALORIES | 2G PROTEIN | 22G CARBOHYDATE 4G TOTAL FAT (2G SATURATED) | 3G FIBER | 0MG CHOLESTEROL | 35MG SODIUM

VANILLA COCOA MIX

Prepare hot cocoa mix as directed in step 1, but add **half of a vanilla bean** (pod and seeds) before blending in processor.

MEXICAN SPICE COCOA MIX

Prepare hot cocoa mix as directed in step 1, but add **2 teaspoons ground cinnamon** and **¼ teaspoon cayenne (ground red) pepper** before blending in processor.

MOCHA COCOA MIX

Prepare hot cocoa mix as directed in step 1, but add **⅓ cup instant coffee powder or granules** before blending in processor.

INDEX

Note: Page numbers in **bold** indicate recipe category lists.

PHOTOGRAPHY CREDITS

Antonio Achilleos: 90
James Baigrie: 13, 14, 21, 32, 39, 40, 44, 47, 57, 60, 63, 73, 83, 95, 96, 100, 109, 110, 120, 122, 129, 145
Mary Ellen Bartley: 86
Monica Buck: 2, 27, 74, 79, 80
Tara Donne: 36, 99, 104, 134
Getty Images: Michael Rosenfeld, 11
Lisa Hubbard: 136, 149
iStock: creacart, 8 (chocolate); Donald Erickson, 8 (chips); iodrakon, 10; Jim Jurica, (salsa); Irena Misevic, 8 (pasta)
Frances Janisch: 6, 133, 141
Yunhee Kim: 142
Rita Maas: 48, 119
Kate Mathis: 22, 77, 103, 114, 130, 138, 150
Ngoc Minh Ngo: 126
Con Poulos: 66, 68
Sarah Reynolds: 106
Kate Sears: 31, 50, 54
Studio D: Jesus Ayala, 8 (can, bowl of beans); Philip Friedman, 7, 35
David Prince: 18

Front Cover: Kate Mathis
Spine: Mary Ellen Bartley
Back Cover (clockwise from top left): Monica Buck, Anna Williams, Tara Donne

METRIC EQUIVALENTS

The recipes that appear in this cookbook use the standard United States method for measuring liquid and dry or solid ingredients (teaspoons, tablespoons, and cups). The information on this chart is provided to help cooks outside the U.S. successfully use these recipes. All equivalents are approximate.

METRIC EQUIVALENTS FOR DIFFERENT TYPES OF INGREDIENTS
A standard cup measure of a dry or solid ingredient will vary in weight depending on the type of ingredient. A standard cup of liquid is the same volume for any type of liquid. Use the following chart when converting standard cup measures to grams (weight) or milliliters (volume).

Standard Cup	Fine Powder (e.g. flour)	Grain (e.g. rice)	Granular (e.g. sugar)	Liquid Solids (e.g. butter)	Liquid (e.g. milk)
1	140 g	150 g	190 g	200 g	240 ml
¾	105 g	113 g	143 g	150 g	180 ml
⅔	93 g	100 g	125 g	133 g	160 ml
½	70 g	75 g	95 g	100 g	120 ml
⅓	47 g	50 g	63 g	67 g	80 ml
¼	35 g	38 g	48 g	50 g	60 ml
⅛	18 g	19 g	24 g	25 g	30 ml

USEFUL EQUIVALENTS FOR LIQUID INGREDIENTS BY VOLUME

¼ tsp	=						1 ml	
½ tsp	=						2 ml	
1 tsp	=						5 ml	
3 tsp	=	1 tbls	=			½ fl oz	=	15 ml	
		2 tbls	=	⅛ cup	=	1 fl oz	=	30 ml	
		4 tbls	=	¼ cup	=	2 fl oz	=	60 ml	
		5⅓ tbls	=	⅓ cup	=	3 fl oz	=	80 ml	
		8 tbls	=	½ cup	=	4 fl oz	=	120 ml	
		10⅔ tbls	=	⅔ cup	=	5 fl oz	=	160 ml	
		12 tbls	=	¾ cup	=	6 fl oz	=	180 ml	
		16 tbls	=	1 cup	=	8 fl oz	=	240 ml	
		1 pt	=	2 cups	=	16 fl oz	=	480 ml	
		1 qt	=	4 cups	=	32 fl oz	=	960 ml	
						33 fl oz	= 1000 ml	= 1 L

USEFUL EQUIVALENTS FOR COOKING/OVEN TEMPERATURES

	Fahrenheit	Celsius	Gas Mark
Freeze Water	32° F	0° C	
Room Temperature	68° F	20° C	
Boil Water	212° F	100° C	
Bake	325° F	160° C	3
	350° F	180° C	4
	375° F	190° C	5
	400° F	200° C	6
	425° F	220° C	7
	450° F	230° C	8
Broil			Grill

USEFUL EQUIVALENTS FOR DRY INGREDIENTS BY WEIGHT
(To convert ounces to grams, multiply the number of ounces by 30.)

1 oz	=	¹⁄₁₆ lb	=	30 g	
2 oz	=	¼ lb	=	120 g	
4 oz	=	½ lb	=	240 g	
8 oz	=	¾ lb	=	360 g	
16 oz	=	1 lb	=	480 g	

USEFUL EQUIVALENTS LENGTH
(To convert inches to centimeters, multiply the number of inches by 2.5.)

1 in	=		2.5 cm
6 in	= ½ ft	=	15 cm
12 in	= 1 ft	=	30 cm
36 in	= 3 ft	= 1 yd	= 90 cm
40 in	=		100 cm = 1 m

THE GOOD HOUSEKEEPING TRIPLE-TEST PROMISE

At *Good Housekeeping*, we want to make sure that every recipe we print works in any oven, with any brand of ingredient, no matter what. That's why, in our test kitchens at the **Good Housekeeping Research Institute**, we go all out: We test each recipe at least three times—and, often, several more times after that.

When a recipe is first developed, one member of our team prepares the dish and we judge it on these criteria: It must be **delicious, family-friendly, healthy,** and **easy to make.**

1 The recipe is then tested several more times to fine-tune the flavor and ease of preparation, always by the same team member, using the same equipment.

2 Next, another team member follows the recipe as written, **varying the brands of ingredients** and **kinds of equipment.** Even the types of stoves we use are changed.

3 A third team member repeats the whole process **using yet another set of equipment** and **alternative ingredients.** By the time the recipes appear on these pages, they are guaranteed to work in any kitchen, including yours. **We promise.**